Here's what people are saying about *Boxing For Everyone*:

"This type of publication is long overdue that makes the "art" of boxing easy, clear, concise and most importantly for everyone. It shows that the art of self defense and the commitment and dedication of those in the sport is paramount. This book celebrates the success of people dedicated to the wonderful sport of boxing."

—Sandy Martinez-Pino, Board of Directors, USA Boxing; World Chair Women's Commission for Amateur International Boxing Assn; Commissioner, New Mexico Athletic Commission.

"There's never been a how-to-box book like this one. Along with solid information on basic techniques, training and equipment, Coach Cappy Kotz speaks directly about the seldom acknowledged doubts and fears the newcomer brings to a strenuous and aggressive sport."

—Katherine Dunn, novelist and boxing reporter

"*Boxing For Everyone* is a welcome addition to our training resource library. Anyone interested in successfully meeting challenges in life, in the ring, or both will benefit from this book."

—Jessica Lawless, founding member of Home Alive

Boxing For

Everyone

How to Get Fit and
Have Fun With Boxing

Cappy Kotz

AmandaLore Publishing, Seattle, Washington

Inside photos by Paul Kotz
Illustration and book design by Chris Wolfe
Production by Joanne De Pue
Cover photo by Adam Crowley
Copy editing by Full Circle Writing and Editing
Additional inside photos by Betsy Bruce

Manufactured in the United States of America

10 9 8 7 6 5 4 3 2 1

AmandaLore Publishing
1111 E Madison, Suite 433, Seattle WA 98122
www.girlbox.com   info@girlbox.com

Publisher's Cataloging-in-Publication
(Provided by Quality Books, Inc.)

Kotz, Cappy, 1955-
        Boxing for everyone : how to get fit and have fun with boxing /
Cappy Kotz. -- 1st ed.
        p. cm.
        Includes index.
        Preassigned LCCN: 97-073685
        ISBN: 0-9657737-9-5

        1. Boxing--Training. 2. Physical fitness. I. Title.

GV1137.6.K68 1998   613.7'11
                                               QBI97-41007

Acknowledgments

I've had the good fortune to work with some great boxers and boxing trainers. I would like to thank Jim Shaver, former Golden Gloves champion; Sandy Gable, whose heavy bag I still use; Robert DiMarco, former Canadian boxing champion; Jonathan Standridge for teaching me how to block a hook; and Ron Paul. I would like to thank Joe V., Job Milton, Bumblebee, Noe Ramirez, Bobby Joe and George Credit; these boxing coaches have passed along great training tips. I appreciate all the boxers I have worked with for providing me with the chance to expand my coaching skills. I especially thank Bob Jarvis for all he has done to help me and to further women's participation in boxing.

I've appreciated working with such talented people on this manual. I want to thank Chris Wolfe and Paul Kotz for their fine work, and Home Alive for lending us their space. Thank you to my mother, Mary Kotz, for helping us get started. Many thanks to Veronica, Karen, David, and Evette. Thanks to my editors, Tom and Sara Pendergast, for their insightful comments. My appreciation to V, Pat, and Phrin for their help.

Disclaimer

In view of the complex, individual, and specific nature of health and fitness problems, this book is not intended to replace professional medical advice. The author and publisher expressly disclaim any responsibility for any liability, loss or risk, personal or otherwise, which is incurred as a consequence, directly or indirectly, of the use and application of any of the contents of this book.

If you do not wish to be bound by the above, you may return this book to the publisher for a full refund.

Contents

About the Author

Cappy Kotz is a fitness trainer and registered boxing coach. She has over twenty years of coaching experience and has led numerous seminars and workshops on achieving goals through boxing. She lives in the Pacific Northwest.

Punching A Heavy Bag Is Like Nothing Else

intro-
duction

Boxing is a kind of conversation, primarily with yourself, and when you spar, a dialogue with your partner.

When I was nine I found a pair of old boxing gloves in the family closet. I filled a burlap bag with hay and started punching. A lifelong boxer was born. Punching on a heavy bag is like nothing else. The surge of power through your limbs is intoxicating. Your body wakes up as the tension built from swallowing hurt or anger, from holding yourself back, is released through exertion. You realize you have more muscles than you generally use. It suddenly makes sense that boxers are at the top of the list when it comes to being fit. Boxing is an excellent conditioning sport that not only builds cardiovascular endurance and muscular strength, but sharpens mental clarity and one's ability to acknowledge and thereby let go of underlying fears. Plus, boxing is fun.

When I was nine boxing programs for girls didn't exist. Even though the gloves I found had been my father's, my family was not sports-minded. Which meant I was on my own. Despite having no instruction, I knew how to strike my makeshift bag with my fists. I pummeled it, reveling in my strength. In this manual I refer to that as gut level

One of the most successful female boxers was Barbara Buttrick, who claimed both the English and European titles in the 1950s.

punching. Gut level punching is when you punch from the gut, letting whatever is inside out. Through training a boxer learns to channel this raw energy into skill. I regret I didn't have any formal training. Without it I didn't even know I had talent that could be developed. But I did have fun that summer. I learned I was strong and that it felt good to exert myself.

I didn't get back into boxing until I was well into my twenties. I was a hot shot by then; I was tough and I was cool. I also had problems managing my temper. I felt like a yo-yo. I played soccer and worked out in a gym, and generally felt good about myself. On the other hand I fought a lot with my intimates. Blowing up at people was how I got rid of accumulated stress, but it made matters worse. I had a hard time controlling my anger. Something would tick me off—I never knew what it would be—and I would fly off the handle. I didn't want therapy because I sensed talking about what I was feeling was not what I needed. I met up with a woman—I will call her Sue—who had a punching bag in her garage. She had done some boxing with her ex-husband. When she suggested we work out together, I jumped at the chance. But the situation didn't last long. After a few lessons from a mutual friend we decided to spar. Sue was cautious; I was not. I still had no clue about technique. From our few lessons I had not learned that boxing is a controlled sport in which emotional reaction has no place. I unleashed everything I had. My pent-up feelings, combined with my fear of being hit, made me wild. Sue ended up with a broken nose. That was a big turning point in my life. I knew I wanted more of the rush I had felt "being in the ring," and I knew that I needed to learn how to have that rush in a way that didn't hurt others or myself.

Around this time I started coaching instead of playing soccer. I discovered I had a talent for coaching. I could see how some players' inefficient movements kept them from reaching their potential. I developed exercises that taught the team soccer skills as well as trained them to move in more efficient ways. Not only was I coaching others, but I coached myself every day using the heavy bag I had put up in my apartment. I learned to feel how I moved and to pinpoint when my movement patterns were not efficient. I trained with ex-boxers and boxing trainers, then went home and broke down the moves I had learned so I could adapt them to my body. I still did gut level punching, too. The difference between my gut level punching and the punching control I learned taught me about emotional management. Every time I went to swing from some inner anger, I could feel my body tightening up, which increased my chances of getting injured. This is when I realized what people have known for centuries: boxing is a discipline that conditions the mental, physical, and emotional self. Because of boxing I am a calmer and gentler person today. Physically I am stronger and more flexible. I continually get leaner due to muscle gain and fat loss. My endurance has increased, and in all parts of my life I am more effective than I used to be.

Boxing is a workout that will last you a lifetime. You do not have to have athletic experience to begin. Each individual trains at a level that suits her capacity for exercise and discipline. Even if you do not box the rest of your life, what you learn in this manual will benefit you. Whatever your goals are, the boxing program I have designed will help you meet them. This manual will show you how. Following are some of the goals you could choose:

- Greater strength

- Conditioning: Cardiovascular strength, toning and weight loss

- Emotional steadiness

- Self confidence

- An ability to defend yourself

- Flexibility and coordination

- Readiness to compete and win

But Where Are The Women?

Boxing has not always been a sport for everyone. In Britain in the 1700s boxing matches were essentially slug fests, which alienated the public from the sport. Then gloves were introduced, and by the turn of the twentieth century there had been repeated efforts by various boxers to bring strategy to the ring, to make the sport more of a science instead of a contest between brutes. Though some mourned the change, boxers began to be appreciated for their finesse and their footwork rather than for their ability to give and take punishment. It wasn't until the middle of the century that it became popular for boxers to be admired for more than their toughness and strength. Muhammad Ali is an example of a boxer who has modeled social conscience, personal integrity, and a keen sense of humanity throughout his career.

But what about the women? Many people are surprised to learn that women have been boxing since the 1800s, though in the United States boxing wasn't recognized as a professional sport for women until the 1970s. More women than ever are stepping into the ring to compete professionally. In 1993, Dallas Malloy won her right in court to compete as an amateur boxer, paving the way for women to register as amateurs with USA Boxing. There are boxercise programs springing up in health clubs and gym facilities across the nation, ranging from purely aerobic-type programs to fitness boxing with or without contact. Boxing gyms are opening their doors to recreational boxers, a term that describes those who want to train but aren't necessarily interested in competing. Now boxing is for everyone.

Christine Filiberto, amateur judge and referee, was the first female to referee at a National Golden Gloves tournament.

Anyone Can Learn To Box!

Both women and men feel the constraints society places on boxing. Women are often encouraged to restrain their physical strength, and are discouraged from hitting. Though aggressive behav-

The author's ninety-nine year old grandmother practices on the heavy bag.

Become better acquainted with your emotional range. Do you tend to be more outwardly aggressive or inwardly timid? Boxing is in part learning how to travel this entire range without getting stuck at any one point.

ior is more readily accepted from men, many men may feel ashamed of being physical or may have bad memories of being bullied by others. Part of boxing is coming past these feelings. The first thing you learn is how to assume your Basic Alignment (BA), a way of positioning the body that aligns you with your center of gravity. This will be your foundation for your boxing technique; it will be something you carry with you wherever you go. As you train with me, you will learn how to box and you will learn how to integrate your new skills and strength into your everyday life.

Since receiving my coaching license with USA (United States Amateur) Boxing, I have worked with boxers who are fighting professionally and with boxers hoping to go pro. I have trained amateur boxers, recreational boxers who spar, and recreational boxers who do not spar. I have worked with boxers who come to me for conditioning, and I have worked with boxers who have turned to boxing to learn stress management. In my club, The Capitol Hill Boxing Club, everyone is welcome. Everyone trains hard. Whether you compete or simply train, my motto is: *training is your trophy*. That means the process is more important than the outcome. When you box with me you are a contender because you will strive to live up to your potential, in life as well as in the ring. Boxers are a special breed: they meet their own limitations and dare to proceed in the face of potential danger, and they strive to get past inhibiting emotions such as anger and doubt in order to perfect their skills. These are skills we all can benefit from and they are skills you can have. Boxing will give you all of this and more.

What This Manual Offers You

This manual covers boxing basics. Each chapter has an introduction that tells you what to expect from that chapter and will illustrate the point with lessons from other boxers' experiences. The first part of the chapter lists the boxing techniques you will be learning. I include photos and illustrations to help you visualize them. The techniques are not complex. Some of them will be more difficult for you than others, but as long as you maintain your BA and keep your mind on being self-aware you will do fine. I've stated each instruction you will carry out in bold type, and for those who prefer more explanation I have added a supplementary description.

Chapter One explains how to assume your BA (Basic Alignment); this chapter is a must for anyone starting her training. **Chapter Two** addresses the boxing stance and explains what being 'on guard' means. **Chapter Three** outlines the main punches that a boxer uses; boxers interested only in training might consider skipping the hooks at first. **Chapter Four** explains how to punch a heavy bag. If you already have a heavy bag you might want to turn to this chapter. It will take you through the steps of hanging your bag, wrapping your hands, and choosing gloves, things you will want to do before you start punching. **Chapter Five** addresses the speed bag. If you do not have one or do not have access to one, skip it for now. **Chapter Six** explains skipping rope; **Chapter Seven** addresses footwork; and **Chapter Eight** outlines stretching techniques. If your body is tight you might want to start with this chapter. **Chapter Nine** provides you with supplemental strengthening techniques; **Chapter Ten** helps you put together a workout that is right for you. You may want to start with this chapter, referring to earlier chapters as you need to know more information. **Chapter Eleven** is about listening to your body. This chapter gives you invaluable information about how to interpret some of the sensations you will encounter while boxing.

After the instructional part of each chapter I have included an **Ask The Coach** section. Here I present some of the questions I have been asked over the years, and suggest possible answers. In the final section, **Things To Think About,** I talk about a variety of things having to do with boxing. It is my aim to supply you with information, enhance your thinking process, delight your senses, and take you through the workout of your life. For your added benefit I have added side bar quotes, bits and pieces of philosophy that help illuminate all of the possibilities you might discover through boxing. You will find in the **Appendix** suggested resources, so you can learn more about boxing on your own. Everything you need to start boxing is in this book.

Basic Alignment

chapter

1

Emotional surges are similar to electrical spikes—they bring the system down. In the case of an emotional surge, one reverts to *old* movement patterns. Assuming BA is like flipping the breaker back on. Once again your system is aligned.

The first thing I teach the boxers who work with me is how to assume Basic Alignment (BA). BA is a way of holding your body which starts with the placement of the feet and extends to the positioning of the hips, shoulders, and arms. Boxing requires precision and strength, which cannot be achieved by exercising on top of old movement patterns that no longer serve you well. Your muscles are meant to function in an efficient manner, but over the years, due to varying circumstances, all of us get out of alignment. When you assume BA you place your body in a state of postural balance in which you are aligned with your center of gravity. BA will not only provide you with a solid foundation for your technique, but it will help keep you injury free.

Every boxer I have worked with has been amazed at how much stronger they feel once they have positioned themselves according to BA. Women in particular tend to hunch their shoulders forward as a way of covering the breasts, which puts stress on the shoulder joints and does not allow for powerful punching. When you assume BA your shoulders are drawn back and dropped, which opens up the chest and allows you to breathe deeper. Naturally you will feel more in command of yourself. The process of drawing the shoulders back and dropping them may make you feel vulnerable since you no longer will be covering yourself up. But as your pectorals or chest muscles develop, this position will feel more normal to you. Your initial sense of vulnerability will be replaced by a feeling of confidence.

The second part of assuming BA is positioning the hips directly under the shoulders. Without realizing it many people, women in particular, tilt their pelvis back, which not only pulls the body out of whack but is detrimental to boxing. Through BA you will be bringing the hips as a unit forward so that they will be directly over your feet and under the newly aligned shoulders. Most boxers I have worked with feel shaky in this position at first. If BA feels odd to you, it's because you are not used to having your pelvis positioned correctly, lined up with your center of gravity. When your pelvis is out of alignment you do not have a solid foundation, a center. Your center is the source of your power, and in boxing, the source of your punches.

In simplest terms, assuming BA is about moving the shoulders back and the hips forward. Then begins the process of strengthening this posture. At first you have to mentally remind yourself to assume BA because your body will continually revert to old habits. With practice BA will become second nature. You cannot practice your BA enough. I ask my boxers to pay attention to their BA not only in the gym but at home and at work, at any time of the day or night. The benefits you get from assuming BA will last you a lifetime because it is the foundation of who you are.

When you are learning how to assume your BA, I suggest you look at yourself in a mirror so you can get used to what your body looks like when it is all lined up. Once your eye can see that your body is lined up, you can check out how you feel in that position. Later, when you are working on technique, you won't always have to look in a mirror. You'll know by feel whether or not you are Basically Aligned.

The difficulty with using a mirror is that we all have insecurities of one sort or another. It is easy, when looking at your own reflection, to get caught up in criticizing what you see. Once you start doing that, however, you are no longer discerning whether or not your body is lined up. If all you can see is how you cannot line up your body, you will never see how you are learning to line it up.

Amateur boxing parallels life in that you need to learn and grow everyday.
—John Brown, Golden Gloves champion and president of Ringside, Inc., *The Boxing Manual*

Good mental form is the releasing of thoughts as they arise, directing your attention to your movements.
—Dan Millman, *The Warrior Athlete*

Therefore, I will remind you often to be **self-aware** instead of self-critical. For instance, when looking in the mirror to see when your hips look aligned, put aside all other thoughts, especially critical ones about yourself. Practicing to be self-aware instead of self-critical is a benefit of boxing that will last a lifetime.

I worked with a boxer who first came into the gym with her shoulders hunched forward in an excessively protective manner. I'll call her Tanya. When I had her assume the Basic Alignment, she found the positioning of her hips relatively easy, but when it came to bringing her shoulders back she had a hard time. Because her shoulders were drawn so far forward, her neck was a source of extreme tension, and when she punched the heavy bag she couldn't punch hard for fear she would hurt herself. I had her maintain BA while she jumped rope, while she practiced her step and jab, while she did everything. As she learned to hold herself more and more through her hips and through the strong muscles of her back, the tension in her shoulders evaporated.

I am always pleased watching boxers like Tanya transform. Inside the gym she went from a timid-acting person to being one of the strongest punchers I have had the fortune to work with. Outside the gym was another matter. Every time she left she reverted to her old alignment. She told me when she tried to maintain BA in her everyday life she felt as if she were showing off, as if she were going around asking for a fight.

Many boxers struggle with such issues. It is one thing to be successful in the ring or in the gym, and another to maintain winning combinations in everyday life. A boxer's success may go to his or her head, making him think he's invincible, the toughest person ever. Or a boxer may feel frightened for having actually claimed her own power. Boxing will change you. You will carry yourself with more confidence as you become stronger and more agile. And you will learn how to manage this change. I suggested to Tanya that she might be feeling afraid she would be attacked for showing strength. She decided to risk this possibility and challenged herself to maintain her BA for an entire day no matter what she felt. The result, she reported, was that people tended to treat her with more respect than usual. And once she started maintaining her BA in and out of the gym, she became a much better boxer.

Look forward to transformative experiences of your own. Boxing brings out the best in you in surprising ways. Get ready to have some fun.

Maintaining and strengthening BASIC ALIGNMENT means abandoning old habits, a process that requires courage and consistency of focus.

Basic Alignment

STEP 1

Stand facing a mirror with feet shoulder width apart.

It can be helpful to use a mirror as a way of seeing what your body is actually doing. Unfortunately it is too easy to become self-critical. Therefore, I suggest you use what I call a soft focus. Instead of glaring at your reflection or critically searching out everything that you do not like about yourself, train your eyes to look for what feels and looks right to you. Every time you get distracted by disliking some part of yourself, remember to switch your focus. Look for something that seems right to you.

STEP 2

Position your feet so the toes point directly forward.

Using a soft focus, look at your feet and make sure they are positioned correctly. Make sure you are standing on the entire foot, distributing your weight evenly between ball, heel, and the two sides.

STEP 3

Bring your hips forward until they are directly over your feet.

Bring the hips forward as one unit until they are over your feet (see figures 1-1 and 1-2). Maintaining this position, turn sideways to the mirror to check the sides of your legs. They should be straight up and down. Think of the sides of your legs as two rods. Remember to keep these rods straight up and down. Look at your knees in the mirror. Are your kneecaps pushed back? If so they

Figure 1-1.
When you are Basically Aligned, your legs will be straight up and down.

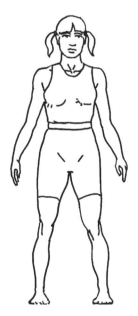

Figure 1-2.
Basic Alignment.

are probably locked (see Chapter Eleven, Listening To Your Body). Bring the kneecaps slightly forward until your knees feel gently flexed and relaxed.

STEP 4

Bring your shoulders back and drop them.

Open up your chest by drawing your shoulders back and dropping them. This may take some getting used to, but eventually your chest muscles will get stronger and your self consciousness and feelings of vulnerability will fade. Your arms hang directly down from the shoulders with the palms facing the body.

STEP 5

Practice the technique.

In order to assume BA you need to know how it feels to be out of alignment. Thus, whenever you feel out of alignment, you will know to automatically assume BA. Standing sideways to the mirror, carefully sway your hips back just enough to feel minor stress in the lower back (see figure 1-3). This is a common posture that puts you out of alignment. Notice how the sides of your legs and your hips are no longer directly over your feet. Now hunch the shoulders, bring them forward and up toward your ears. Pay attention to what this feels like for a few moments. This feeling is your signal to assume BA. Bring your hips forward as a unit until they are over your feet, with your toes pointed forward. Bring the shoulders back and drop them, allowing the arms to hang down in a relaxed fashion, palms turned toward the body.

Let us go through the procedure again. Assume BA. Check your feet. Are they lined up, toes pointed forward? Now bring your hips forward

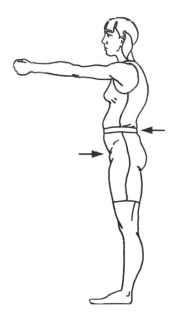

Figure 1-3.
Out of alignment.

(see figure 1-1) so that they are over your feet and the sides of your legs are straight up and down. Draw the shoulders back and drop them. You might feel a little shaky at this point. Until you get used to it, this position feels strange. Think of the sides of your torso as two up and down rods. This will help you maintain your torso as a unit. Take a moment to be aware of your back. It connects your two side rods. Boxers get their quickness and power when they move from their back forward. You want your stomach to feel pleasantly tight, not pooched out or sucked in. If your lower back hurts, you are probably tilting your pelvis to the rear. Gently align it forward. You will need to reaffirm all alignments from time to time because your body will automatically revert to old habits.

Ask the Coach

This alignment stuff makes me feel out of whack.

Switching over from old habits to a boxer's stance will feel strange at first. Remember to practice this technique: go back and forth between aligned and unaligned so you'll know the difference and will be better able to reaffirm your BA when you feel out of alignment. Two indicators that signal you to assume BA are:

- Pain in the lower back, which indicates the pelvis is tilted back and the torso isn't being maintained as a connected unit between shoulders and hips;

- Pain in the knees could indicate your pelvis is tilted back.

I'm amazed how much BA opens me up, but, I swear, I can't move when I'm like that!

Your old alignment may have had you pitched forward on your toes, causing you to hold yourself in your knees and lead with your shoulders, whereas BA is going to open you up to move from the back of your body forward. Give it time. Every boxer has to learn about maintaining a more empowering stance and building her punches and footwork from there.

I feel fine maintaining my BA, except when I visit my family. They don't understand why I want to box, and I end up reverting to my old posture so I won't threaten them. What should I do?

You're daring to be stronger, and that is never as easy as it should be. In a way your family is a chance for you to practice being in the ring. When you are in the ring, your opponent will do her best to knock you off balance, which challenges you to remain balanced and stick to your technique. When you visit your family, you don't need to talk about boxing, but by the very fact of maintaining your BA you will be living it.

The point is—and this is necessary to understand the difference between male and female athletes—that in the arena men take for granted the fact that they are males and concentrate on being athletes. Women never forget that they are females.
—Dick Lacey

Things to Think About

Remember to be self-aware instead of self-critical when you practice your BA in the mirror. You are not looking for where you are too fat or too skinny, for how weak you look or even how amazing you are. You're watching for the moment when your hips move forward as a unit, when your shoulders move into an opened position.

Work your hips. Bring one up while keeping the other one down. Put one forward and the other back. The angle of your belt line or the waist of your pants will tell you if your hips are tilted one up and one down, or are tilted one back and one forward. When you have assumed your BA, the waist of your pants should be level. Do the same with your shoulders, make them go in opposite directions. Then align them in matching positions, back and down. How does that make your chest look and feel?

Boxing will change your body. Just assuming BA will change your body. This position puts your muscles into their proper alignment. As you work out, this muscular alignment will replace your current shape with a leaner, more compact look. In a way learning to box is a kind of self-sculpting. In order for boxers to do all the quick, smooth moves that they utilize in the ring, they have to be exceedingly flexible. Flexibility comes from stretching and strengthening all muscles, which in turn brings your actual shape tighter to the bone. This compactness is what gives a boxer's punch its snap, gives her the ability to step in quick with the jab.

Working your hips and shoulders as a unit might take a while. Keep on reaffirming your BA as many times as you can during a day. And not just when you are standing around, either. See what you can do to maintain your BA when you reach down to lift something. Take a moment before getting in and out of chairs to find your BA.

Think about this: anyone who has trained, who performs her sport, will take home with her the shape of that performance. The way a boxer holds herself indicates to what extent she has strengthened her muscles and to what extent she has the use of them in the ring. That is why I encourage my boxers to work both ends of the spectrum. Train hard in the gym and be aware of using your new, emerging, sleeker shape in your everyday life.

On Guard

When your training feels tedious or boring, assume you have checked out and are just going through the motions. Either renew your focus or cease exercising until you experience genuine interest once again.

On guard refers to the ready position a boxer assumes during training or in the ring. It is a combination of BA (Basic Alignment), the boxer's stance, and dynamic tension.

I discussed BA in Chapter One. A boxer's stance is a positioning of the feet and hands. The feet are staggered and the hands are held up high, ready to protect the face. Publicity shots of boxers generally show them in their stance. The boxing gym where I work has a lot of photos on its walls of boxers who have passed through the gym at one time or another. They are portraits of courage and daring. Though the positioning of the feet and hands is largely the same in each photo, each boxer is different. As boxers mature they develop their own style. Some boxers adopt a tough-looking stance, others are more casual about the way they stand. They all look very fit and ready to box. Some of the boxers look out from behind their fists while others prefer to look over the top. A boxer's stance is important. Without it she becomes disoriented. Every technique you will learn will be from your stance. Your stance becomes your home.

Those who stay with boxing learn about focus, heart, and dedication.

The third element of being on guard is dynamic tension. Everyone reacts in times of stress by either readying to fight or to take flight. A boxer learns to control these reactions, to harness that energy for her own use. She also learns to relax overly tight muscles while maintaining an alert tension throughout her body. This is readiness, a state of dynamic tension, of being on guard.

A cat cannot help but always be on guard. When something startles her she takes action in less than an instant. People have lost this ability. Not only have our lifestyles become sedentary, but our actions are often restricted by our own fears. A boxer knows about fear. When he gets in the ring he will either want to flee or attack. But if he starts backpedaling and defending, the body becomes constricted and shut down. If he launches an attack he will find himself off balance and out of control. Either reaction uses energy, and the boxer will quickly become exhausted. A boxer's goal is to stay centered and, when he is hit by a surge of adrenalin, to harness that impulse by focusing on BA.

Out of the ring, assuming BA in place of reacting with inappropriate anger, for instance, will give you time to respond instead of react. In the ring, assuming BA when you might feel discouraged and defeated allows you to return to your center of gravity, both emotionally and physically. Once you have your center you have your moves. Boxers practice all of their techniques from their stance, and your stance is based on BA. In the face of emotional reactions respond by assuming BA because that centers you in your stance and allows you to use technique. Thus, the energy involved in having a reaction has not been dissipated but turned into dynamic tension. You are ready and on guard, directing your punches at will.

You already know how to practice self-awareness while looking in the mirror. You tell yourself to return to your chosen focus when critical thoughts try to take over. In that instance you have chosen dynamic tension. Your awareness is sharpened as you seek to attain your focus. Telling yourself to do this is a mental action. The physical part comes when you do what your mind has asked. Back and forth you will go, telling yourself and doing, telling yourself and doing. Eventually this process will get easier, and then it will become instinctual. A boxer needs her instincts, for they allow her to sense a punch before it hits and to know how her opponent will move even before she does.

Learning begins with awareness. Being aware means learning to see the "weak" parts of oneself as an occasion to get stronger.

Some of the most profound effects of making the techniques instinctual come when you experience duress. Even though this manual does not cover sparring, I often refer to sparring because,

Boxing gives you inner strength.

competitive or not, you will be training your body, mind, and emotions to function as a smooth unit under times of duress. If you decide to spar, master the basics first. Being able to tap dynamic tension, a feeling of allover alertness, will make your workouts more fun. See yourself as your own best opponent. Use your mind to note when you are no longer focused on the task at hand. Revert to BA, resume your stance, and then you can get back to technique. Remember, when the going gets rough you will either want to leave or get mad. Always seek the midpoint which is center.

One year I put together a women's boxing event. We packed people in and still had to turn them away at the door. We started out the event with demonstrations of various boxing skills. One boxer skipped rope while another two did medicine ball drills. There were examples of shadowboxing, and then sparring matches for the second half of the show. The boxers who sparred were recreational boxers; therefore, the matches were not contests. I was the referee. As I had expected, there were few fouls for me to call. Everyone who trains with me trains hard, and those boxers were good at their technique. What is difficult to prepare for is how boxing in front of an audience will affect you. Though we had worked on emotional management, how to turn reaction into dynamic tension, when the boxers got in front of the crowd they all struggled to retain their BA in the face of intense urges to either fight or flee. Those who went into fighting mode escalated their intensity but lost track of their skills, and those who went into flight mode collapsed against the onslaught. As their coach, it was my job to insist they assume their BA, thereby regaining their stance and technique. The crowd particularly enjoyed when a boxer regained her center and ability just when it seemed she might lose it. It was a high energy, fun-packed evening.

Afterwards I asked the boxers what they had learned. One boxer—I'll call her Babs—had always exhibited cockiness in the gym. She said, "I never understood before how much I have to be on guard against my own fear. I always thought I would be fine in the ring, but I ended up dealing with my own reactions rather than actually boxing."

For Babs, the cocky boxer, being tough had always been enough. No matter what happened she assumed a tough attitude. That was her code. It worked. People like tough, and she was charmingly good at it. It served her well. But when she got in the ring for the first time outside of practice, she realized that tough wasn't enough. In fact she needed her BA and her technique much more. She approached her workouts differently after that. It wasn't that she stopped being tough. Instead she learned to be tough about pouring her cockiness into BA. She learned to be on guard for emotional reactions as a signal she was losing touch with her skills.

Think you're ready? On guard.

Taking Your Stance

STEP 1

Assume BA, stand with feet shoulder width apart.

These steps are for the right-handed boxer. Left-handed boxers need to reverse hands and feet.

STEP 2

Slide your left foot to the right so your left toes touch the right toes.

Slide your left foot over so your left toes meet your right toes at an angle (see figure 2-1). The hardest part about assuming your stance will be maintaining your BA at the same time. You will end up with your feet being staggered, which may throw off your sense of how to keep your hips forward as a unit. Be patient. Each change feels strange at first.

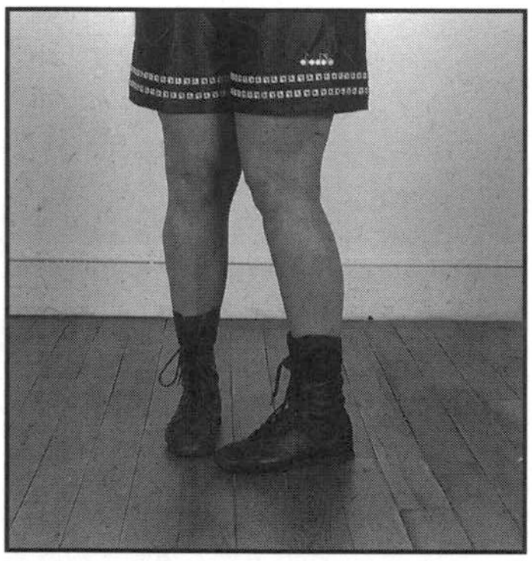

STEP 3

Move your left foot directly forward about twelve to fifteen inches.

Step forward with your left foot so that your feet end up being staggered, approximately twelve to fifteen inches apart (see figure 2-2). The toes of your front foot will be pointed somewhere between 12 and 2 o'clock. The rear heel is raised slightly off the floor, with the toes also pointed somewhere between 12 and 2 o'clock. Check out your hips in the mirror. Even though your feet are staggered, your hips remain level. (Look at your waist line. When your hips are level the waist of your pants will be level.) Keep your hips directly under your opened shoulders and directly over a midpoint between your feet. It is more important than ever to experience your torso as a unit. Think of your sides as two rods and make sure they are straight up and down, connected by your back.

STEP 4

Make a fist with the left hand, place it level with your left cheek.

Your left hand is carried in front of your left cheek, with the palm side facing the face (see

Figure 2-1.
When taking your stance, touch the toes of your left foot to your right foot.

Figure 2-2.
The correct foot position for a right handed boxer.

figure 2-3). Make a fist by loosely curling your fingers so the tips touch the palms of your hands. Your thumbs cross in front of the fist so they rest against the middle finger's knuckle.

STEP 5

Place your right fist level with chin.

The right hand is carried level with the chin (see figure 2-3). Reaffirm your BA. Part of being on guard is your ability to keep your hands up in the correct position. Be aware that keeping your hands up may cause your shoulders to come back up around your ears. Your shoulders are meant to rest on top of the torso with the weight of the arms gently keeping them down.

Proponents of boxing characterize it as 'the noble art of self-defense,' the 'sweet science,' a channel for courage, determination, and self-discipline—the sport which, above all others, combines fitness with skill, strength with artistry.
—Jennifer Hargreaves, *Boxer: An Anthology of Writings on Boxing and Visual Culture*

Figure 2-3.
A right handed boxer's stance.

STEP 6
Practice the technique.

Assume BA and then your stance. Go back and forth several times from standing with feet shoulder width apart to the staggered position of your stance until you feel comfortable with the correct placement of your feet. Remember to keep the heel of the rear foot slightly off the floor when you are in your stance, equally distributing your weight between both feet. Make sure you are not tipped forward onto the balls of your feet. If you are, sink more of your weight down through your arches and heels. Keep your elbows pressed in toward your body. Remember to breathe, deep from your diaphragm. Check the position of your hands and make sure your thumbs are on the outside of the fist, not on top, not inside. Hold your muscles lightly tensed, in ready position. Every time some distracting thought comes into your mind revert your attention to reaffirming your BA. This is your on guard position, otherwise known as your stance.

Ask the Coach

Where should my elbows go?

Keep them in close to your ribs.

Every time I try to feel alert and ready for action, like you said, I can feel myself reverting to my old alignment habits. My shoulders come forward as if to protect me, my hips go back as if I'm trying to get away, and then I have to start all over again.

Maintaining your BA while you're assuming a dynamic stance can be tricky at first. That's a boxer's training, to keep to one's center even when the brain is sending fight or flight signals to the body.

I keep forward on my toes. Is that right?

You want to be ready to move from the back of the body; therefore, you don't want to be tipped up on your toes. Instead hold yourself up with the imaginary rods on either side of your torso. Remember your back connects those rods. Lightly clench your butt muscles. They are very strong, so use them. If your belly sags forward, gently press your back forward over your hips until you can feel your back supporting you.

Things to Think About

Do not forget your feet. You are already maintaining BA as you walk through life. Now bring an added awareness to pushing back through the rear foot at the end of each stride (see figure 2-4). Get used to pushing against the ground through your leg and foot. When you start punching you will need to access that sensation of pushing against the floor. This connection to the ground will keep you from literally throwing yourself into the punch. With both feet contacting the floor, you will always know where you are. It is not uncommon for boxers, when they first start training, not to know where their feet are,

Figure 2-4.
As you walk be conscious of pushing back against the ground through the rear foot.

whether the toes are pointed forward or to the side, whether the heel is raised, or even if the foot is lifted entirely off the floor. You can gain more awareness about using your feet when you walk. Generally place your feet heel to toe with each step. Maintain your BA and try to move forward through the back rather than tipping forward by falling into and clenching with the knees.

As you walk be conscious of pushing back against the ground through the rear foot. Keep your balance. A boxer's punches are not going to be effective if she is always getting thrown off balance. Pay attention to times when your weight is distributed on one foot more than the other and times when the distribution is equal. This is something you can do while standing in line. We all get plenty of experience standing in lines! Quietly assume BA. No one needs to know this is what you are doing. When you feel like your feet are lined up, toes pointing forward, slightly flex your knees. Bring the hips forward, connecting the sides of your legs from foot to hip in straight lines. From your practice watching in the mirror, you will know what your legs feel like when they are straight. Subtly draw the shoulders back and down, lining the sides of your torso straight up and down. Remember to breathe. Pay attention to your feet; distribute your weight equally between them. Be conscious of the balls, arches, and heels as well as the inside and outside of the foot. We all have a tendency to rest our weight more on one area than another. Distribute the weight equally to all parts of the feet. If you are correcting long standing habits of foot misalignment, you may have to press hard to use a part of your foot you do not generally use (see Chapter Eleven, Listening To The Body). Ever so subtly shift your weight so most of it rests on the left foot. Reverse the direction and shift your weight onto your right foot. Pay attention to how your muscles shift to accommodate the transition without losing balance. Are you still maintaining BA?

A skilled boxer learns to lightly shift his weight, to remain balanced while slipping punches and landing his own. You too will have this ability. And to think it all began while standing in line.

Figure 2-5.
On Guard.

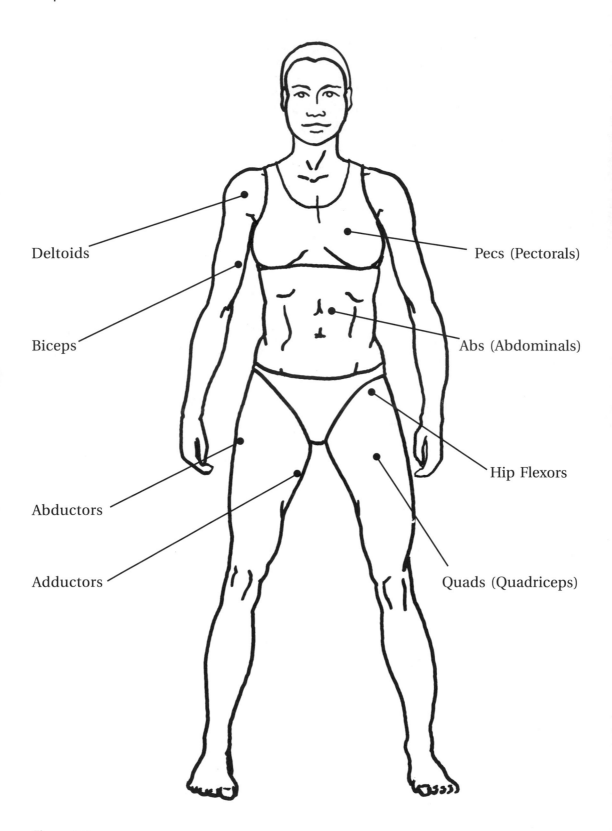

Deltoids

Pecs (Pectorals)

Biceps

Abs (Abdominals)

Abductors

Hip Flexors

Adductors

Quads (Quadriceps)

Figure 2-6.
Muscles, front view.

©1998 Cappy Kotz   Boxing For Everyone: How to Get Fit and Have Fun With Boxing

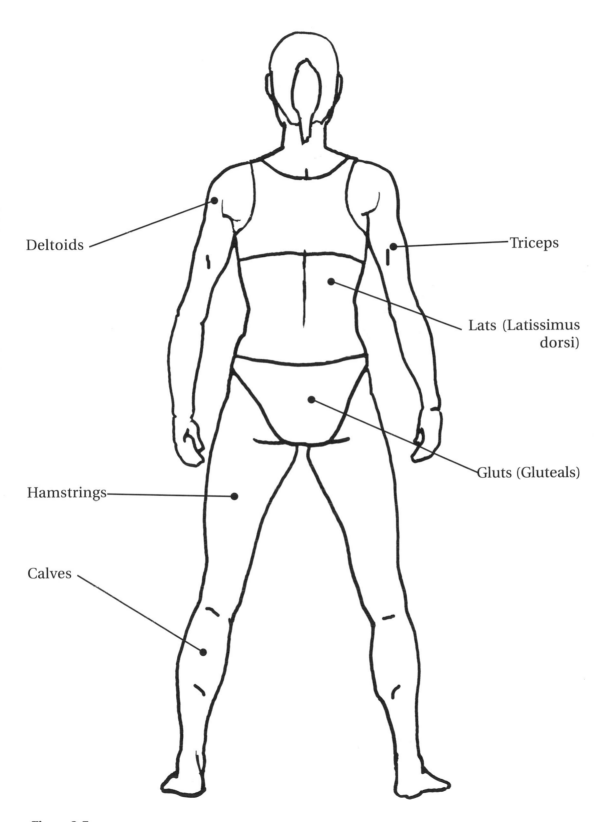

Deltoids

Triceps

Lats (Latissimus dorsi)

Gluts (Gluteals)

Hamstrings

Calves

Figure 2-7.
Muscles, back view.

©1998 Cappy Kotz   Boxing For Everyone: How to Get Fit and Have Fun With Boxing

Straight Punches
and Hooks

The perfect hook was first used by the mama bear defending her young.

The intention of a punch is to be effective. In professional boxing an effective punch evades the opponent's defense and either makes a clean point, stuns the opponent, or knocks him down. In amateur boxing an effective punch also evades the opponent's defense and makes a clean point, hopefully taxing the opponent in some way. In aerobic or fitness boxing the punch technique is used to work and tone the body while burning off calories and excess fat. In this situation an effective punch will be one that travels its correct and most efficient path. Recreational boxers may or may not spar. The ones who do are concerned with their punches being quick, controlled, and powerful. Recreational boxers who do not spar are largely concerned with proper technique so they can punch a heavy bag without injury.

Basically there are three types of punches. Straight punches, true to their name, travel along a straight, horizontal path between you and your target. You will learn two straight punches. When you take your stance, your forward hand is your jab, while the rear hand delivers a straight right. (Straight left for left-handed people.) Just as your feet do not change position when you are in your

You have weight and you have the means of launching that weight into fast motion.
—Jack Dempsey,
Championship Fighting

stance, your hands also remain the same. The left hand, carried level with your left cheek, is always used for the jab, while the right hand, carried level with the chin, is your power hand. A straight right is considered your power punch.

Think of a channel the width of your shoulders and the length of your extended arm between you and a sparring partner. Your straight punches must stay within these boundaries to tap their ultimate power. This is accomplished by keeping your elbows in close to your body as you deliver the punch. Each time you send a punch through this channel, you bring it back on the same plane. This keeps your punches in a straight line, out and back, which is the quickest, most efficient route.

Your jab is the more active of your straight punches because it has various uses. You use the jab to gauge the distance between you and your sparring partner. Sometimes the jab is a quick snap, almost a tease, other times it is a no-non-sense blow. Not only is it used to set up other punches and punch combinations, but also throwing a constant jab is a good way to keep your opponent off you. It has lots of uses, and therefore should be practiced over and over until it flicks out as easy and as commanding as a whip.

The straight right is the punch that waits for an opening that you have set up with your jab. The straight right has longer to travel than the jab and, unlike the jab, is similar in intensity every time. Bam. Line your body up. Put your weight behind it. Push back against the floor. Let it go. The classic one, two, is a quick jab and a straight right. One, TWO. Turn that fist over at the last second so the underside of the knuckles face the floor at point of contact. It is that quick rotation of the fist that provides a final explosion of power.

The second kind of punch, the hook, is different from a straight punch because it is a bent arm

punch. The force of it travels laterally in front of
you. The power is generated through a move
referred to as a body whirl. This technique takes
getting used to, so be patient. The hook is well
worth all the time you put into it. It is a powerful,
highly satisfying punch. When you smack a hook
into the bag with all of your body weight behind
it, you will know what I mean. Practicing your
hooks will build your lats (basically the muscles
along the sides of your body). Learning to use
your lats is one of the best parts about boxing.
They are tremendously powerful, useful muscles.
I didn't discover mine until I was in my twenties,
and I have been eagerly developing them ever
since. Girls are not generally encouraged to use
their lats. Many boys also grow up feeling a lack
of upper body strength, or are timid about assert-
ing themselves. Part of timidity is not having
access to the lats. These muscles help shape your
torso, help give your posture a vote of confidence.
So practice those hooks and build your lats.

The third kind of punch is the uppercut. It is a
vertical punch delivered upwards to the underside

> When your combinations start
> to come together, when you
> feel the fluid movement
> behind all your practice, that is
> when boxing really begins.

The power of the punch is not in the muscle of the arm as much as in the weight and form of the body.
—Rene Denfeld, *Kill The Body The Head Will Fall.*

of your opponent's chin. This punch is best learned after you have mastered the basics and is not covered in this manual.

I worked with a boxer once—I will call him Stan—who had low self esteem. Stan wanted to box because he felt this would give him more confidence. I started him off learning his BA (Basic Alignment) and his stance, and as soon as he learned how to punch he started in on the heavy bag. All those years of feeling he couldn't make an impact, feeling he didn't measure up to other guys, were forgotten as he pounded the bag. Every week he came to the gym he walked a little taller, with a little more spring to his step. His shoulders started filling out, and he began liking how he looked. After he had been boxing six months, he felt he was ready for light sparring, an experience he never thought he would have. I told him he didn't have enough control to spar yet. So he worked harder, which meant he tried to punch even harder than he already did. But punching harder isn't the way to become a better boxer.

The problem was Stan didn't actually know how hard he could hit. He was so accustomed to thinking of himself as physically puny he couldn't perceive himself as having the kind of strength that could hurt someone. That was the reason it would have been dangerous to have him spar. I explained to him that effective punches come from technique and encouraged him to pay more attention to correct alignment. He tried but he couldn't get past his idea that to punch harder meant he would be stronger. He ended up straining one of his shoulders and with a strained shoulder he couldn't punch the heavy bag. Not punching the bag meant a loss of all he had hoped for, the chance to be strong and confident within his body. I told him if he focused on maintaining his BA (Basic Alignment) and structuring his punches from there, he would attain his goals.

As you learn to punch remember that power ultimately comes from your center, and the way to access that power is to perfect your technique. Instead of trying to punch harder, pay more attention to how you deliver your punches. Think of punching or projecting your punches through your target rather than attacking or punching at your target. As Stan learned to punch from his center, he realized how much energy he normally used defending himself, trying to convince himself he was strong. Now he uses that energy to fuel his punches, which in turn has given him a sense of control. Not only has he started sparring, but he has a more consistent experience of inner confidence than ever before.

You are going to have this kind of control and power, too. I will take you through your punches in this chapter. Practice them. They are your tools.

The punch is not a push, nor does it come from the shoulder, but is to be a release of intent from your center. Your arm is the vehicle of this force and must be trained to remain solid without breaking.

The Jab

STEP 1

Assume Your Stance.

Go through the entire routine of assuming BA and your stance until this process is natural, something you do not have to think about. Remember, the jab is always thrown with your forward hand. (Left-handers, remember you reverse your feet and hands.)

STEP 2

Shift your weight onto your right leg.

Shift the majority of your weight onto your right leg (see figure 3-1). This provides a counterbalancing effect.

Figure 3-1.
Before you jab, shift your weight onto your right leg.

STEP 3

Punch with your jab, rotating hand just before you reach full extension.

A punch is an extension of your arm (see figure 3-2). The goal is to make contact with your target through your fist or glove. Just before you strike your target, rotate your hand so your thumb faces the floor. Keep those wrists straight! If you strike a heavy bag with a bent wrist, you can easily injure yourself. (Review Chapter Four, Punching a Heavy Bag.) Use more of those imaginary rods to splint your wrist so it will not bend. Keep your elbow tight to the body and slightly flexed at point of impact.

STEP 4

Bring the left hand back to original position.

The punch is delivered and returns on one plane. No weaving up and down or side to side. You may want to watch your punch in the mirror to make sure it is a straight punch. Keep your elbow slightly flexed at full extension. Otherwise you might hyperextend it. Do not let your shoulder lead, causing you to bend from the waist to make your punch. Keep your shoulder back, maintain your torso and hips as a unit. If you practice in the mirror, you will obviously not have a target to strike. Still, imagine you are striking one. This will help you keep your dynamic tension intact.

STEP 5

Practice the technique.

In the mirror see what it looks like when you punch with the shoulder. Exaggerate punching with the shoulder, bunch it up, make it be the momentum behind your punch. Now resume BA, keep your left shoulder back and

Figure 3-2.
The Left Jab.

down. Imagine the flow of the punch coming from your midsection. When you deliver your jab, keep your punch anchored by lightly contracting your back and butt muscles. This way you will be less likely to fall into the punch.

Stepping with the Jab

STEP 1

Take your stance.

Practice this technique in the mirror. When moving it is easy to lose connection with your BA. Continually remind yourself to maintain BA.

STEP 2

Jab, stepping forward with your lead foot at the same time.

Punch with your left hand at the same time you step forward with your left foot (see figure 3-3). Your fist should reach its full extension as your forward foot contacts the floor. Keep the elbow slightly flexed and punch through the second knuckle. The fist at the moment of impact is rotated so the underside of the knuckles face the floor. Your weight is primarily distributed to your right leg. (Left-handers reverse legs.) To step with your jab is to step into a sparring partner's space, delivering a punch to their face. Even if you are just practicing this in the mirror, keep alert. Remembering the

Figure 3-3.
Stepping with the jab.

intention behind this punch will help you maintain dynamic tension.

STEP 3

Your punch returns as your rear foot moves into correct stance position.

 As your jab returns ON THE SAME PLANE, bring your rear foot up so that once again your feet are in their correct stance, slightly more than shoulder width apart. Continually check your feet to make sure your stance does not get too narrow. Your fist returns to its position level with your left cheek, knuckles once again turned to face your cheek.

Figure 3-4.
A straight right punch: The power hand.

STEP 4

Practice the technique.

Step without punching with your jab. Step forward with your left foot, maintaining BA. Now bring up your rear foot to the point where you have resumed your stance. Continue advancing until this is comfortable. Remember to think about stepping into someone's space. There's heightened tension involved in that. You are committing yourself to a potential risk. Now add your punch so the step and punch happen simultaneously. It is a slightly explosive gesture.

Power Hand: The Straight Right

STEP 1

Assume your stance; shift weight to left leg.

After you assume BA and then your stance, shift your weight to the left leg. (The reverse for left-handed boxers.)

STEP 2

Straighten the right foot so toes point forward as you punch with your right hand.

Maintaining the majority of your weight on your left leg, pivot the rear foot so that the toes are pointed directly forward. At the same time deliver your right punch, pushing back against the floor with your rear foot, and pushing the right butt forward so that your right hip flexor (basically the front of your hip) flattens. Rotate the fist at the last second so that your thumb is facing the floor (see figure 3-4).

STEP 3

Bring right hand back to original position.

Bring your hand back on the same plane the punch was delivered on. Your rear foot will resume its original position, with the toes pointing anywhere from 12 to 2 o'clock.

STEP 4

Practice the technique.

As a way of remembering NOT to lean your body into the punch by bending from the waist, do it a couple of times to see what it feels like. Bend from the waist and punch from the shoulder. Look in the mirror. Can you see how your torso moves forward off your hips? Now resume your BA and maintain it. Do the straight right correctly. Shift your weight to the left leg, pivot the rear foot so the toes point forward and at the same time deliver the punch. If you want more reach push your right hip forward from the butt. Look in the mirror. Make sure your hips are over a midpoint between your feet and that your torso is over your hips and under your shoulders.

Anger, fear, defensiveness, and shame are a few of the many emotional reactions we experience in any given moment that obstruct our flow of energy.

Left Hook

STEP 1

Assume your stance.

You are preparing to do a bent arm punch. Clear your mind from thinking about straight punches. Focus instead on a channel that travels laterally in front of you. You will be sending the force of your hooks along this channel.

STEP 2

Raise your elbows, touching your fists together at mid-chest level, palms toward your chest.

First you will practice the body whirl. Assume BA and then your stance. Place your fists against your chest, the palms turned toward the chest (see figure 3-5). Check out the weight distribution of your feet. At this point it should be equal.

STEP 3

Whirl your body to the right, pivoting your left foot so your left toes point at your right foot. Your left elbow stops at a midpoint in front of you.

Take the time to break this move down. You are in your stance, weight evenly distributed between both feet. Now shift your weight to your right leg while at the same time whirling or rotating the body to the right by pivoting on the ball of the left foot so the toes end up pointing at the right foot. This movement will automatically bring your arm along with it (see figure 3-6). Stop when your elbow reaches a midpoint in front of you. First practice this in the mirror so you can check out the placement of your feet. Then try it on the heavy bag so that your elbow strikes the surface of the bag.

STEP 4:

Assume your stance. Whirl your body to the right as before but ending with the left arm in a ninety degree angle, fist stopping at a midpoint in front of you.

Break this move down again. Assume BA and then your stance. Distribute your weight evenly be-

Figure 3-5.
The ready stance for the body whirl.

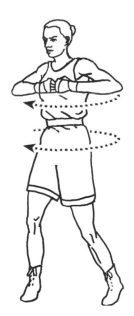

Figure 3-6.
Body whirl to the right.

tween both feet. Shift your weight to the right foot as you pivot on the ball of your left foot. Whirl the body to the right so that the left toes end up pointing toward the right foot. At the last moment, snap the left arm up into a ninety degree angle. Your left fist stops at a midpoint in front of you (see figure 3-7). It is a lateral punch. The force of it comes from the body whirl and from your left foot pushing back against the floor. The left side of your torso should be facing the direction of the punch. Practice this move over and over. Make sure your left foot pivots so the toes point toward the right foot. This encourages the left hip to whirl to the right.

STEP 5
Return to your stance.

Smoothly pivot your left foot back to its original position. Your left fist returns to its position level with your left cheek, knuckles turned toward the face. Reaffirm your BA. Check that your feet are in their correct position.

STEP 6
Practice the technique.

Practice the left hook one part at a time. First the feet. Shift your weight and pivot on the ball of your left foot. This means your left heel is off the floor. Do it over and over until it is smooth. Look in the mirror. Are your hip and left torso coming all the way around? Do your left toes end up pointing toward your right foot? Mentally picture what you are doing and try it again. Now practice the elbow technique. Whirl to the right so you get a feeling for how the arm comes right along with the movement. You do not have to make a hook happen. As long as you whirl the body correctly, the punch comes along for the ride. Finally, do the body whirl, bringing the left arm into a ninety

Figure 3-7.
The left hook.

degree angle at the last second. In the mirror your fist should stop at a midpoint in front of you. On the bag, your fist strikes the side of the bag. In a sparring match a hook would be directed either at the side of your sparring partner's torso or at the side of her head.

Right Hook

STEP 1

Assume stance.

Remember if you are left-handed, reverse all directions. The right hook is the same as the left hook except you are whirling the other way. Take a moment to review the steps you followed delivering the left hook. Mentally picture how you would do these same directions but as applied to a right hook. Picture whirling the right side of the body toward the left, and pivoting the right foot.

STEP 2

Begin with the elbow strike. Whirl the body to the left, pivoting the right foot so the right toes point at left foot.

Assume your BA and then your stance. Place your fists together against your chest, with the palms turned toward the chest. Equally distribute your weight between both feet. As you shift your weight to your left leg, whirl the body to the left, lifting the heel of your right foot and pivoting on the ball. Your right toes will end up pointing toward your left foot. This pivot may not feel as easy as the left hook pivot. This is because your right foot is further back. Concentrate on getting the right hip well forward. Mentally push it forward from the back of the butt. Your elbow will end up striking a midpoint in front of you.

STEP 3

Complete the right hook. Whirl the body to the left, substituting the right fist for the elbow strike.

Shift your weight onto your left leg as you whirl your body to the left, pivoting the right foot so the toes end up pointing at the left foot. At the last second snap the right arm into a ninety degree angle (see figure 3-8). The fist strikes the side of the heavy bag or stops at a midpoint in front of you if you are practicing in front of the mirror. The fist should be in an up and down position. Check that your right hip is well forward with the right side of your torso lined up on top. Push back against the floor through the ball of the right foot for more power.

Figure 3-8.
A right hook.

STEP 4

Practice the technique.

Be patient; no one has learned how to execute a hook in a day. Break the move down, practice each part over and over. The body whirl takes some getting used to. Start in the strike position, with either the elbow or fist against the bag. Check out your feet and make sure they are correct. Make sure that the foot on the same side as the hooking arm is pivoted. Now bring that same hip forward. Mentally push the butt forward which will consequently push the hip forward. Your hip flexor should feel flat rather than concave. Push off the pivoted foot, which will push the body forward and your fist or elbow into the heavy bag. Resume your stance and try it again.

Ask the Coach

How can I keep from being self-critical when I look in the mirror? All I can see is how big my hips are. They will never be anything but two big lumps.

Think of practicing in the mirror as a sparring session. You're seeking effectiveness. Getting distracted by emotional reactions to what you see isn't the kind of effectiveness we're talking about. Remember, the hardest part is getting through the awkward stage. Look in the mirror, be aware of where you feel tight. In this case be aware of your hips. You said they are big lumps. OK, they are big lumps. It's not their fault or your fault. More important is that you need looser hips in order to punch more effectively. Be persistent, gently push them forward into alignment by assuming BA in your stance. Here comes the reaction, don't get distracted, slip the feeling, keep thinking of bringing your hips and torso forward as a unit. Be alert for any tiny sensation of release or that you understand what I'm talking about. Stay with it, stay in the ring, you've got to be tough to get through this. Keep your focus, and there! Did you feel it, that little shift that happened? Did you see that? I know it's minuscule, but don't get caught up in feeling hopeless. You are not in training to feel hopeless. Learning to align your body under your punch for ultimate effectiveness is like learning to walk: it takes practice. A baby doesn't give up because she can't do it the first time, does she? That's what 'training is your trophy' means: seeking satisfaction in the doing of it instead of wishing you were already there.

I get off balance when I step and jab.

The trick to moving is remembering you are moving your center. You are not stepping first or moving your shoulders first, but moving through space through your hips. So when you step forward, don't let yourself hurry up and get there faster. Stay over your hips. Initiate the move with your hips, then step and punch at the same time. When you catch your rear foot up, remember not to overstep. Keep a slightly more than shoulder width gap between your feet when you are on guard.

Now that I understand the body whirl, I practice my hooks all the time. They are powerful! What I want to know is what kind of punches do the cowboys use on old Westerns? Their bodies whirl around but their arms are not bent.

The punches you are referring to are haymakers, basically a wild swing. In the ring this kind of maneuver would leave you wide open. A hook can be a wide hook, which will result in the arm being less bent. Sometimes I have my boxers try haymaker-type swings so that they can get a sense of what the hooking action feels like. When you do these kind of swings, your arm completes a circular motion all the way around your body. That is what your hooks should feel like. Even though your fist stops at midpoint, the whirling action should feel as if the arm had kept on going around the body.

Things to Think About

Boxing means something different to everyone. When you tell people you are a boxer, they may or may not have a reaction. Some people consider boxing a brutal sport, while others view it as a discipline that integrates the body and the mind. Each person has to decide for herself what boxing means. Your thoughts on the subject will change as you become more involved with boxing. I started boxing as a kid because it felt good. I returned to it again when I was in my twenties because it made me feel tough and strong. By the time I was in my thirties, boxing became a way of learning more about my unconscious self—my fears, hurt, anger, and grief. It was during this time that I realized I needed to learn about emotional management. Now I am in my forties, and boxing is an integral part of my life. My workouts are more challenging and rewarding than when I started. I am also coaching, offering others the opportunity to train, a chance I wish I'd had when I was nine and eager to learn.

The first time putting on a pair of gloves, punching a heavy bag, getting the feel of a hook, is great. The first time in the ring is scary and exhilarating. As in any other discipline, a boxer's training moves in a spiral. There are the learning curves, which involve repetition and new challenge, and there are the times when everything comes together and you feel your body and mind functioning as one.

The consistent factor throughout is the fact that boxing, at whatever level, involves punching. Punching is a form of hitting. You wrap your hands and hit a heavy bag. You work on your techniques, imagining a sparring partner, even if you are not planning on getting in the ring. A real or imaginary sparring partner provides that edge, makes you understand there is a purpose to how you step and line up your punches.

Many women have a hard time even thinking about punching others. Boxing is about technique: the better your skills the less likely it is you will inadvertently get hurt or hurt others. Punching a heavy bag is an excellent way to better understand what punching or hitting means to you. I have a boxer whose main focus in learning to box is getting out her anger. She works on her alignment and technique in the mirror, then "spars" with the heavy bag. Each week the heavy bag represents a different person who, during the week, she has felt mistreated her. A heavy bag is not a person. You can punch it as hard as you can without hurting it. When you experiment with punching as hard as you can, you quickly discover all sort of things about yourself. For instance, you might realize where your technique could be stronger. You might realize you stop breathing when you act in an aggressive, assertive manner. You will definitely come to appreciate all the complexities involved in hitting, or in your case, punching.

Punching a Heavy Bag

chapter

4

When expelling air as you punch the heavy bag, experiment with letting out sounds in a low voice. The lower down in your register your voice comes from, the more you will tap the aggressive part of you.

There are different kinds of punching bags. A heavy bag, weighing between forty and one hundred fifty pounds, is one of them. When you work out on a heavy bag, you get a chance to exert your power. It feels good to punch hard. As long as you maintain good form you will not get injured. Each time you connect with a solid punch, the force of your blow reverberates back through your muscles making them stronger and strengthening your confidence, too. Punching provides you with the experience of being effective.

Athletic stores generally sell forty, sixty, or eighty pound heavy bags. Boxing gyms tend to have one hundred to one hundred fifty pound heavy bags. The lighter a punching bag is the more it moves around when you strike it. Lighter bags are good for practicing precision and control. The heavier bags move around less, which means you can pound on them without them swinging out of range. The surface of heavy bags is either vinyl, canvas, or leather. You use gloves when you punch, so you do not have to be concerned with whether or not the surface material will be hard on your hands. You do want to be concerned with the contents of a heavy bag. Water filled bags do not hurt your hands, but some boxers feel that the impact of their punches evaporates when they work out on a water filled bag. Rag or sand filled bags are solid, and they provide a wonderful return power-jolt to your muscles, but the contents can clump up and form hard lumps that could damage your knuckles. Boxing gyms mostly have soft filled bags. These bags have been lined with thick foam to help prevent injury. If you work out at a boxing gym, you should have no problem with troublesome bags. If you buy your own bag, ones that are softer offer more protection.

Before you work out on a heavy bag, you need to purchase handwraps and gloves. As with any boxing equipment, you can usually get most of what you need at athletic stores, or you can order a Ringside catalog (see the Appendix). Some handwraps are made from a heavy cotton and others are made from a stretchy material that provides a more contoured fit. Both kinds secure with Velcro. As for gloves, get the laceless kind, either with an elastic cuff or the kind that secures with Velcro.

Handwraps and gloves protect your hands. As I said in Chapter Three, keep your wrists straight at the moment of impact so you do not strain them. And you want your elbows to be slightly flexed when your glove strikes the bag. This keeps them from hyperextending. Alignment is everything. If you get your body in the correct position, the force of the punch explodes through you into the heavy bag.

When you work out on a heavy bag, you will be working on two things: technique and gut level punching. Technique is learned through repetition. Your jab will not come to you overnight, just as the hooks and the straight right will need to be perfected. Repetition paves the way for instinct. It is the same with your BA (Basic Alignment). The more you practice being aware of it, the more it will begin to be your natural way of being. But technique is not everything. Doing the same punch over and over can get stale if you do not actually "feel" it. Your punches have to mean something else besides whether or not they have been done correctly. This is where gut level punching comes in.

Punching at a target reinforces the idea of going for a goal 100%.

Gut level punching is a way of getting more content into your punches. Taking care to keep your wrists straight (and I mean splinting them with imaginary rods so they DO NOT BEND) and your elbows slightly flexed, punch the heavy bag with all the energy you have. When you gut level

A sturdy eyebolt screwed into a beam, ceiling stud or door frame is strong enough to hold a punching bag.

punch, you are not concerned with form or if your punches are correct. Just keep the wrists straight because when you punch as hard as you can, you will tend to be wild. For some people gut level punching will be difficult because it is about letting go, about letting whatever is inside come out in a punching flurry. When you get tired or feel uncertain how to continue, return to technique. For others, technique will be difficult and the repetition will quickly become boring. When this happens return to gut level punching. Everyone needs to practice both.

Working out on a heavy bag is a dialogue with yourself. The connection of your punch against the bag tells you how much impact you have had. When the bag swings out of control, you have to control it. You are responsible for keeping your wrists and elbows safe when you go all out. You feel your body getting stronger and more confident. Stress and tension evaporate after a couple rounds of punching. From head to toe you will feel like a new person.

I told you about my first punching bag, the one I made when I was nine. I was given my second punching bag fifteen years later. I belonged to a women's gym, and when the owners could no longer keep up their lease and were forced to close, they asked me if I would like to have their lone punching bag. I had worked out on it three times a week from the time the gym opened and, since no one else had showed much interest in it, I guess the owners felt it should be mine. I accepted and, not having a car at the time, hoisted the sixty pound bag onto my shoulder and walked it home, twenty-five blocks. That was a good workout! Not only physically, but I got plenty of practice sticking to my focus when a few people leaned out their window to stare. When I arrived home, I screwed an eyebolt into a ceiling stud and hung my new "roommate" up. (Later, when I moved out of my apartment I filled the hole in with spackle and no one ever knew the difference.) At last I could punch whenever I wanted. Since then I have always had a punching bag in my home. I practice technique on my bag and I punch to music as a way of getting my feelings out. I punch to relieve stress. I work on stabilizing pre-injurious conditions through punch alignment. I work on my BA through punching, and I let friends and family use the bag for similar reasons. Having a heavy bag in your life is a wonderful thing.

Hanging the Bag

STEP 1

Drill a hole in a ceiling stud, door frame, or beam.

If you do not have a drill, borrow or buy one. Use a bit that is smaller than the eyebolt you have chosen.

STEP 2

Screw an eyebolt into the hole.

You can buy eyebolts at a hardware store. Get one with a longer rather than shorter shaft. Screw the eyebolt into the hole you have drilled. Putting a screwdriver into the eye of the bolt, turn it like a handle.

STEP 3

Hang the bag from the eyebolt and tape all "S" hooks.

Your punching bag will come with a chain and swivel. The chain connects to the bag at four different places by means of an S hook. These hooks look like an S. Once you have hooked all four of them onto the bag, secure them with sturdy duct tape. This will prevent the S hooks from coming undone while you are punching. At the top of the chain and swivel is another S hook. Hook this into your eyebolt and secure with tape (see figure 4-1).

STEP 4
Other options.

You can buy free standing frames to hang a heavy bag from. You can also hang a bag from a sturdy chin up bar that you place in a doorway. You do not need lots and lots of room. If all you have is a small, narrow place, your punches will be limited, but it is better than nothing. The advantage to a confined space is that you have to learn control. If you have a basement or a garage, consider yourself lucky.

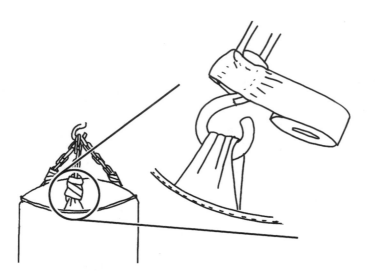

Figure 4-1.
When hanging a heavy bag, tape all S hooks.

Wrapping Your Hands

STEP 1
Hook the loop over your thumb.

Unroll your handwraps. You will have two, one for each hand. Place one of the loops over your thumb, keeping your fingers slightly spread (see figure 4-2).

STEP 2

Wrap your wrist, palm and knuckles in that order. Repeat.

Keeping your fingers slightly spread and maintaining a steady tension on the wrap, wind the handwrap several times around the wrist. Then wrap around your palm, ending up by wrapping around your knuckles (see figure 4-3). Repeat this order until you have used up the wraps.

STEP 3

Secure with the Velcro strip, and then wrap the other hand.

When you have secured the Velcro strip, make a fist. If you kept your fingers slightly spread as you wrapped your hand, you should be able to make a fist easily. If there is not enough room to make a fist, wrap your hand again. You want your wraps to feel tight, but you do not want them to cut off your circulation. When you have wrapped both hands, they should look neat and tidy (see figure 4-4).

Figure 4-2.
Place the loop of your handwrap over your thumb.

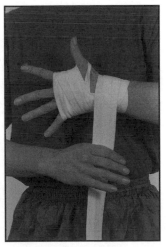

Figure 4-3.
Wrap twice around your wrist, then wrap around your palm and your knuckles. Repeat.

Figure 4-4.
An example of hands wrapped neat and tidy.

STEP 4
Practice the technique.

You do not want your wraps so tight they cut off your circulation, nor do you want them so loose they fall off. If you buy the longer wraps you will want to bring the wrap between each finger and around the thumb. Each one of these steps is followed by bringing the wrap around the wrist to keep it secure. Finish wrapping your hands so they look neat and tidy. Take pride in how you prepare and protect your hands. A boxer with messy handwraps looks like someone who doesn't know what she is doing.

Choosing Gloves

Get laceless gloves either with elastic or Velcro wrists. Bag gloves are less padded and cannot be used for sparring (see figure 4-5). Training gloves weigh between eight to sixteen ounces (see figure 4-6). The more they weigh the more padding they have. More padding is better protection.

Figure 4-5.
Bag gloves.

Figure 4-6.
Examples of laceless gloves. One has an elastic wrist and the other secures with Velcro.

When considering which gloves are right for you, consider how they fit and how much they weigh. You want gloves that do not constrict your hands. You also do not want your hands to swim around inside your gloves.

Heavy Bag Technique

STEP 1

Extend your jab so your glove is in correct position against the bag. Make sure your wrist is straight. Do the same with your right hand.

Once you have wrapped your hands, put your gloves on. Extend your jab so that your glove is in contact with the heavy bag. Check to make sure you are maintaining BA, that you are in your stance and your feet and hands are in the correct position. (Review Chapter Three on how to punch.) Make sure your wrists are straight. Straight means they are not flexed down, bent up, or turned to either side. Punch the bag lightly with your jab, getting used to keeping your wrist straight and your elbow slightly flexed each time you make contact. Practice doing the same thing with your other hand.

STEP 2

When you connect with the heavy bag, exhale sharply through your nose or mouth.

Each time you punch make a small "blowing out" noise from either nose or mouth. This helps you remember to breathe, and actually puts a little

If you want extra padding for your knuckles, place a sponge or piece of foam over them before you wrap your hands.

more force behind your punch. When you are gut level punching, make a louder noise. This will encourage you to punch from the inside out.

STEP 3
Practice the technique.

First of all, remember that the heavy bag is yours to control. As long as you pay attention to keeping your wrists straight and your elbows slightly flexed, you should not get hurt. Try out each punch technique until you are familiar with how each one meets the bag. Straight punches hit it straight on, while hooks connect with the bag from either side. Think of punching through the bag instead of punching at the bag. Go for power. You want to be effective. Be careful when switching over to gut level punching to make sure your wrists and elbows are prepared to make the adjustment, too. Remember to exhale sharply with each punch. It is easy to stop breathing when you are trying to concentrate. Above all else, have fun when you are punching a heavy bag. It is there for you to enjoy.

What helped me develop quickness was fear. I think the rougher the opponent the quicker I am.

—Sugar Ray Leonard

Ask the Coach

I have noticed boxers use different colored gloves. Does it matter what color I get?

Generally gloves are red or black. You can also get blue and white, red and white, and gloves that are the colors of the U.S. or Mexican flag, to mention a few. What color you get is up to you.

My friend has a forty-pound bag she said she would give me. But I'm a pretty big person. Would that bag be too small for me?

If you are getting it for free, go ahead and accept. You can always get a heavier bag later on. Smaller bags are a little harder to control because they swing around more. If you work out with a buddy, you can take turns holding the bag for one another. If you work out alone, you will get used to controlling the bag. For instance, if the bag swings to the right, stop it with a right hook and vice versa.

I bought a heavy bag and hung it up in my bedroom. I'm really into punching it, and I can't believe how quickly I've gotten lots stronger. But is it normal to feel bigger than I really am? Sometimes after I've punched on the bag I feel taller, like I take up more space than usual. Is that possible?

What you are probably experiencing is one of the benefits of punching a heavy bag. Sometimes life can beat us down a little and punching does restore you to your actual size. Keep up the good work and try assuming your BA when you feel like that so you will retain this feeling longer.

Things to Think About

If you do not have a lot of money, do not buy a lot of gear. Ask at a local athletic store if they might be having an upcoming sale on their boxing equipment. Check the Yellow Pages for second hand sporting goods stores. Sometimes they have good deals. Yard sales, Goodwill, and other thrift stores are places you might find used boxing equipment. Ask friends and family if anyone has a pair of old gloves or a heavy bag. Buy equipment according to what you can afford.

If you want to compete, most boxing gyms provide you with equipment. You may or may not have to pay dues depending on the gym. If you take lessons at a gym, usually the equipment is provided also. You will find that gym gloves can be pretty stinky, so you might want to invest in your own. You will definitely need your own handwraps whether you take lessons, train for competition, or work out on your own.

You do not have to have boxing shoes. Any kind of athletic shoe will do. The surface of a boxing shoe is slick, helping you glide better when you are doing your footwork. The thing about boxing shoes is that they do not have much arch support. If you do get a pair, make a special effort to strengthen your feet (see Chapter Eleven for tips on strengthening feet).

Boxing clothes are fun. Lots of stores carry a line of boxing clothing, even for women. There are great Everlast brand shirts, shorts, and sweatshirts. They make wonderful presents. If your birthday is coming up, tell everyone that is what they should get you. But you do not need boxing clothes to box. Preferably wear clothing that is tighter to your body rather than loose and flowing. It is hard to see if you are maintaining BA if your clothing is really loose. On the other hand, some people find it difficult to look at themselves in clothing that doesn't hide their bodies. Take it a bit at a time. Replacing self-criticism with self-awareness is a thinking process.

The Speed Bag

When you try too hard you restrict your ability to breathe.

A speed bag is a punching bag that is used for perfecting eye and hand coordination. Speed bags come in various sizes, with the smallest providing the hardest workout because it is faster and more difficult to control. The largest of the speed bags is approximately fourteen inches long. Speed bags are made with stitched leather and come with a bladder that you fill up with air. The hardware they come with consists of a metal plate and a hook and swivel that screws into the metal plate. The metal plate is screwed onto a wooden backboard mounted to the wall or a ceiling beam. The speed bag has a leather loop on one end that is slipped over the hook. Speed bags come with or without backboards. If you get one without a backboard, it is easy to make one out of plywood.

When you face a speed bag, the bottom of it should hang level with your nose or your forehead. If it is too high, stand on a platform. Most gyms have their speed bags set up so their backboards can be adjusted. Or they provide platforms you can stand on. Either wear just your handwraps or put on a pair of bag gloves (see Chapter Four for information on gloves). Hitting a speed bag is not very hard on your hands, so minimal protection is all you need.

Boxing is about being direct. It cuts through the superficial and addresses the core.

Strike the speed bag with a backhand punch and the same punch you use on a heavy bag. A backhand punch means you strike the bag with the meaty part of your fist that is directly below your little finger. You hold your fist at an angle and strike the side of the bag close to its bottom edge. When struck, it swings away from you and hits the backboard. Its momentum carries it forward where it hits the backboard, carries it back again, and as it comes forward one more time you strike it. The rhythm is: you hit the bag, it strikes the backboard three times, then you hit the bag again.

Since the speed bag hangs from a swivel, it wants to spin in circles instead of swinging back and forth. Using the two punches I mentioned, you learn how to strike the bag from different angles. This keeps it from going in circles. How hard you hit the speed bag also affects your ability to keep the bag under control. You may see other boxers hitting the speed bag with lots of force. You can add more power once you have mastered the rhythm. To begin, strike the speed bag with medium force.

You want to be able to work the speed bag with both hands. Learn one hand at a time. Then you can alternate them, striking the bag with one and then the other. This creates a mesmerizing rhythm that feels great. When you are in the rhythm, your coordination comes without effort. Eventually the rhythm affects your feet, and you will find yourself moving and stepping in time with your punches. There's a boxer in the gym where I coach whose speed bag work is an art form. His hands move in a fluid blur as he steps, slips, and shimmies to a beat that any drummer would be proud of. What inspires me the most about his speed bag skill is how much he enjoys it. His entire body expresses the fun he is having. It is true, you get more benefit from your workouts if you enjoy them.

Because the speed bag hangs level with your face, you have to hold your hands up. And because the speed bag moves as fast as it does, you do not get a chance to bring your hands down for a rest. This provides you with a chance to work your lats. Initially you will be tempted to hold your arms up by bringing your shoulders up. As you get used to maintaining your BA (Basic Alignment), you will learn to keep your arms up primarily with your lats. That way your shoulders do not get as tired, and you will be practicing correct form.

The boxer fashions her own style out of clumsy beginnings and a healthy dose of fear.

If you have the chance to work on a speed bag at a gym, do not be intimidated by the fact that you cannot do the rhythm at first. I have worked with boxers who felt embarrassed to try a speed bag because they felt clumsy. Everyone has to learn how to work with a speed bag. That means everyone is clumsy to begin with. You get past that stage fairly quickly. It is true that boxers are admired for their speed bag skill. Like the guy at my gym, it is not uncommon for other boxers to stop what they are doing to watch. But that does not mean you will be judged because you do not know how. Boxers are respectful people. They respect the effort it takes to become good.

Hitting the Speed Bag

STEP 1

Stand in front of the bag with your fists in front of your face.

The bottom of the bag should be level with either your forehead or your nose. Adjust the height of the backboard if you can or stand on a platform. Hold both of your hands up.

STEP 2

Strike the side of the speed bag near its bottom edge with the side of your hand, referred to as a backhand punch.

Strike the lower portion of the speed bag with the meaty part of your hand just below your little finger (see figure 5-1). This is a backhand punch.

STEP 3

Allow the speed bag to strike the backboard three times, then strike it again.

When you first strike it, the speed bag will go away from you and strike the backboard. Allow it to swing forwards and hit, then swing and hit the back of the backboard once again. As it rebounds off the backboard begin your punch, striking the lower portion of the speed bag using a backhand or straight punch (see figure 5-2).

Figure 5-1.
Striking the speed bag with a backhand punch.

STEP 4

Follow the same procedure using the right hand.

Remember to stand up tall with your shoulders in their correct BA position. Use your lats to hold your arms up. Relax your neck (see Chapter Eleven, Listening To The Body). And be patient. The speed bag will act as if it has a mind of its own. It will either go in circles, or it will barely move at all. Experiment with hitting it harder if it does not move and softer if it goes in circles.

Boxing is not about hurting others or getting hurt. It is more about learning to let go of one's own insecurities and inadequate self image.

STEP 5

For a two-handed rhythm, strike the speed bag once with the left fist, and bringing the right fist up behind and over the top of the left, strike the bag with the right.

Strike the speed bag first with the left fist. During the time it takes the bag to hit the backboard three times, circle your right fist behind and over the top of the left fist. As the right fist comes over the top of your left it is in position to strike the bag. Continuing in this rhythm, the left fist continues under, behind and over the right, striking the bag, the right circles up, behind and over the left, etc.

STEP 6

Strike the speed bag five times with the left, five times with the right, then alternate hands, striking once with each. Repeat.

You have three rhythms. You can use the left hand separately while the right hand remains stationary. You can use the right while the left remains stationary. And you can alternate hands, circling them up, behind, and over the

Figure 5-2.
As the speed bag comes off the backboard, strike it with a straight punch.

other before they strike. To get used to combining these rhythms, start by striking the speed bag five times with the left. Then strike the bag five times with the right, followed by ten strikes in an alternating pattern of left, right, left, right, etc. Repeat.

STEP 7
Practice the technique.

Learn to hit the speed bag one hand at a time. You will probably be more coordinated with one of them. Be patient with the less coordinated hand until you are proficient with both. Vary how hard you hit the bag. Also, vary when you hit the bag. Ideally you want to start your punch the moment the speed bag leaves the backboard. Use both a straight punch and the backhand punch. The backhand puts a bit of a spin on the bag which helps keep the bag from circling, and the straight punch keeps the bag swinging back and forth. Remember, if your shoulders hurt, use your lats to hold up your arms instead.

Be aware of details such as how you place your feet upon the floor. Can you feel your feet? It is better to know you cannot actually feel them than it is to act as if you do.

Ask the Coach

You weren't kidding when you said the speed bag has a mind of its own. How do I get it to stop going in circles?

Don't muscle the bag. Strike it firmly with medium strength. As the bag comes off the backboard, strike it with your knuckles, keeping your punch level and to the center of the bag. When you use a backhand punch, either strike the bag in the center of the lower portion or slightly to the side. When you strike to either side, you are correcting the bag from going in a circle. Most important, try not to think about it. Once you understand that you strike the speed bag once for every three times it hits the backboard, work toward keeping the rhythm by watching the bag. You will get it.

I either hit the bag too hard or not hard enough. I can't seem to get a consistent pattern going.

When you strike the bag with the correct amount of force, pay attention to how much you used. Then strike the speed bag again with the same force. Don't be concerned at first with striking the bag once for every three times it hits the backboard. Practice getting a consistent amount of force before attempting the rhythm.

I have seen boxers working on the speed bag. Do some of them strike it more than once for every three times the bag hits the backboard?

Yes. Once you have mastered the one for every three rhythm, advance to hitting it one for one. You strike the bag each time it comes off the backboard. Practice one hand at a time, then alternate.

Things to Think About

Punching a speed bag is different than punching a heavy bag. You use a short range punch with the speed bag. Your arm makes a punching motion that is part chop. Some trainers do not approve of using a speed bag, because you do not punch a speed bag the way you punch a heavy bag. Nor are the punches you use on a speed bag punches you use in the ring. I consider speed bag technique a wonderful skill to have. It is a good way to experience rhythmic punching. Even if the punches are partly a chopping motion with the forearm, it is a punching rhythm. Once you get a feel for releasing one punch after the other, you will have an easier time creating punching combinations later on.

Eye and hand coordination is an important skill. Learning to sight the target and follow up with your punch takes practice. A heavy bag provides a big surface to hit, so it doesn't really work your eye and hand coordination. Hitting a small target is good practice. That is how you learn precision. Precision is about placing your punches, using just the right amount of power and angle to make for a clean blow. A heavy bag gives back a jolt, a speed bag does not. Work out on both of them. Sharpen your reflexes with a speed bag and strengthen your body with the heavy bag.

Skipping Rope

Maintain interest in discovering what new level you are about to experience.

Skipping rope burns off fat. The jump rope is flicked up over the head and under the feet with the wrists while the muscles of the arms, chest, back, and shoulders maintain the continuous motion. The boxer's legs, feet, and ankles keep time with the rope, setting a pace that works the cardiovascular system. The faster the boxer skips, the more of a workout it is. Fifteen minutes of skipping rope is one of the best workouts there is.

There are different kinds of ropes to choose from. The rope can be cotton, leather, or plastic. Cotton is lighter in weight; therefore, it doesn't move through the air as snappily as leather or plastic. I prefer leather because it responds better to my guidance. Hard plastic ropes are noisier when they strike the floor, but they also do not wear out.

The weight of the rope is important. Just as the cotton rope has a tendency to float through the air, there are jump ropes on the market that are meant to give you a better workout by being heavier. Heavier ropes can put excessive stress on the forearms. You want to be able to turn your rope easily with small flicks of your wrists. If turning

The qualities that you admire in others are the very qualities you should encourage in yourself, and the qualities you dislike in others are the qualities in yourself you most need to look at.

your rope makes you forearms burn, try a lighter one.

Some jump ropes come with ballbearings in the handles. They allow the rope to turn freely with each rotation. Jump ropes without ballbearings work fine, too. It is up to you. I suggest you try them both to see which one you prefer. The handles themselves can be wood or a plastic mold. The plastic handles come plain or with padded grips. Even though I have had wooden handles crack, I prefer a jump rope with wooden handles. Sometimes padded grips are not made well, and they rip or quickly wear away. The plastic handles without padded grips do not absorb sweat. Handles are also either weighted or not. I recommend getting handles that are not weighted because, once again, a heavier rope can put undue stress on your arms.

Skipping rope is a coordinated effort of the mind, body, heart, and lungs. It is an endurance builder and also an excellent way to warm up. I have my boxers start their workouts by jumping rope. The consistent rhythm demands their attention, which helps get their mind off their day and into their workout. At the same time the rhythm is calming, it is also tiring. This can be used toward warming up. Getting on past minor fatigue helps a boxer focus her mind and takes her to a new level of strength. As you get better at skipping rope, the process will energize you, not only because of oxygen intake, but also because it gets you relaxed and ready for the rest of your workout.

I worked with a boxer—I will call her Lisa—who prided herself on her jump rope technique. She quickly mastered the two-footed step and the boxer's step, then went on to master fancier moves. She would burst into flurries of crossing the rope, jumping backward, and other complicated rhythms. Her stamina was not that great, so she tended to burn out quickly, but she continued to do the flashier jump rope methods because, I think, they made her feel accomplished. I've seen other boxers do flashy routines, incorporating full squats, dance moves, and other intricate footwork. Remember, slow and steady wins the race. Flashy jump rope techniques are impressive but they do not necessarily improve your boxing.

I was in the gym one afternoon when an ex-boxer of local renown dropped by. He had retained good muscle tone from all the years he had worked out, but at the age of fifty-eight he had slowed down and wasn't as fast or flexible as he used to be. He got to talking to me about jump rope technique and to illustrate how he used to train, he grabbed a jump rope and started skipping. He dropped thirty years in an instant as his feet became nimble and his body remembered the fluid moves of timing the rope. He skipped forwards and backward, side to side, even from a crouch. I was impressed with how he had incorporated his boxing moves into his jump rope routine. While watching him, I understood that there is a huge difference between being flashy and having skill.

What you get from practicing a technique is what you put into it. If you practice skipping rope to be impressive, you will know how to be impressive. If you practice it as a tool for getting in better shape, for learning stamina and finer muscle

Boxers face their own fears, knowing that their skills can not fully develop otherwise.

control, it will always be a skill that will take you to higher levels of boxing ability. When Lisa came into the gym again, I asked her to do her skipping rope routine using the two steps I describe later in this chapter. I wanted her to get more out of her practice than the surface excitement of having been amazing, even if just for a moment. She had a difficult time sticking to the basic steps. I could see her working to control her impulses to "perform" more complicated steps. Over a period of time she settled deeper into the rhythm of the boxer's step. Her work in the ring settled down; she became less showy as she developed more combinations that had purpose behind them instead of being just for show. There came a time when she did expand her skipping rope routine again to incorporate more moves. Her approach was different than before. She broke the moves down, figured out how she could use them to get stronger and more agile. And when she practiced them, she did it for herself, not to impress others.

Using a Jump Rope

STEP 1

Standing on your rope, check to make sure the handles come up to your armpits. This is the correct length.

Before you start skipping rope, make sure your rope is the right length for you (see figure 6-1). Stand on the rope and draw both handles up toward your armpits. Adjust the rope so each side is the same length. If the handles reach higher than your armpits, the rope is too long. You can shorten it by tying a knot first on one side and then on the other. If the rope is too short, get another one.

STEP 2
Assume BA (Basic Alignment).

Maintaining your BA while skipping rope will help you get the most you can out of this technique. Especially focus on using the sides of the body (the lats) to keep your torso erect while you skip.

STEP 3
Beginning with the rope behind you, bring it up over your head and under your feet, lifting your feet just enough to clear the rope.

Holding the handles of the rope loosely in your hands, begin with the rope lying on the floor behind you. Your arms should be angled away from the body at the elbows. Making circular movements with your wrists, bring the rope in a loop over the head. Maintaining the loop, bring it down in front of you, jumping over it when it strikes the floor. The feet should come off the floor just enough to clear the rope (see figure 6-2).

STEP 4
Use the two-footed step. Jump over the rope with both feet at the same time, distributing your weight evenly between them.

Jump once for each rotation. Use both feet, distributing your weight evenly between them. Remind yourself to assume your BA often because your shoulders will naturally tend to come forward as you concentrate on swinging the rope around and around.

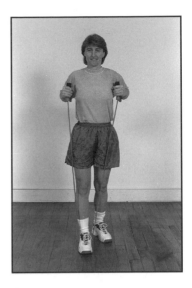

Figure 6-1.
Your jump rope is the correct height for you if the handles come to your armpits when you are standing on the middle of the rope.

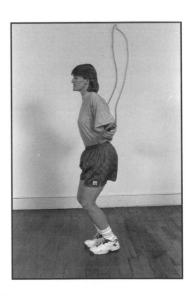

Figure 6-2.
Come off of the floor just enough to clear the rope.

STEP 5

Use the boxer's shuffle. When you jump over the rope land with most of your weight distributed to one foot. Switch your weight to the other foot on the next jump. Continue.

Jump once for each rotation of the rope. When you land bring most of your weight down on the left foot. The ball and toes of your right foot touch the floor to help balance you. The next time you jump switch your weight to the right foot, with the ball and toes of your left foot lightly touching the floor for balance. Continue, switching your weight from foot to foot. Mix up the rhythm, land twice in a row on the right, twice in a row on the left. The rhythm possibilities are endless.

STEP 6

If you get tired, swing the rope from side to side without jumping until you are ready to jump again.

If you do get tired, instead of stopping altogether, continue your rhythm by bringing your hands together, swinging the rope first to one side of you and then the other side. Shift your weight from foot to foot, following the direction of the rope (see figure 6-3). Focus on assuming BA, and when you are ready, resume jumping.

STEP 7

Practice the technique.

Everyone is at different levels when it comes to skipping rope. If you step on the rope, practice being self-aware instead of self-critical. Resume jumping. No matter how many times you "mess up," be patient. It may take you awhile to get the rhythm. Start with the two-footed step. Remember, one jump for each rotation of the rope. People

Figure 6-3.
When you get tired, keep moving. Swing your rope side to side until you are rested.

often start skipping rope with an extra hop for each rotation. Keep track of your BA. Your posture while you jump is important. Keep your shoulders back and down; use your wrists and lower arms to turn the rope. Keep your elbows close to your sides. When you feel comfortable with the two-footed step, use the boxer's shuffle, shifting your weight from one foot to the other. Still use one jump for every rotation of the rope. And if you get tired, keep moving; maintain the rhythm by swinging the rope from side to side. Use this side to side rhythm as many times as you need to, especially if you get flustered because you step on the rope. While you are swinging the rope side to side, calm your mind, return to BA and find the rhythm. Sometimes it helps to count how many jumps you accomplish in a row. That way you will know when you improve. If you feel you have mastered both the two-footed step and the boxer's shuffle, pick up the pace. Burn off that fat; condition your cardiovascular system; get fit!

Don't forget to breathe.

Ask the Coach

Skipping rope is harder than I thought. I want to get better at it, but the rope keeps catching on my feet.

Sometimes you think you are bringing your feet off the floor just enough to clear the rope, when in actuality one foot might be dangling, or flopping to the side when you jump. Try flexing your knees a little bit, and make sure you don't get going too fast. Also, if your arms are held too far forward, the rope will have a greater tendency to hit your legs. Remember to keep your shoulders back and down.

My shins hurt when I skip rope.

Possibly you are landing on your toes, keeping your weight pitched forward onto the front of your body. Hold yourself from your butt, hips, back and sides. When you jump, think of lifting up from your center instead of having to lift your legs. When you land, direct your weight down through your heels without going flat-footed.

I'm not sure where to look when I skip rope. Should I look at my feet?

Good question. I suggest you look straight ahead or slightly upwards. If you look down at your feet, you will bring the shoulders forward which tends to tangle the rope, and you will pitch your weight to the front of your body. Let your eyes go to a soft focus, so you are not exactly looking at anything. You want to be more aware of your BA and trying to get a feel for the rhythm of skipping rope.

Things to Think About

You want to pace yourself. This means working out at a level that is interesting, challenging, and allows you to have fun. If you are bored you are not working hard enough. Pick up the pace. If you feel overwhelmed, slow the pace down. Swing the rope rhythmically side to side until you are ready to jump. Keep your jump rope routine interesting and challenging, and try to use the muscles along the backs of your legs.

Comparing yourself to others cuts into your workout time. Instead of focusing on your BA, you end up focusing on why your body doesn't look like someone else's. Your body may or may not look like someone else's. It doesn't matter. When you compare yourself with others, you either end up being self-critical or critical of others. Be patient. Learning to substitute self-awareness for self-critical thoughts takes time. Knowing that comparing your progress with the progress of others can lead to being critical, switch to BA whenever you feel tempted to compare.

Thinking you are better than others is useless. Boxers who get in the ring know they cannot depend on being better than their opponent. The best you can hope for is knowing how to handle yourself—remembering to use your technique—no matter what happens. Comparisons to others seems like an easy way to know if we should work harder or if we have worked enough. It will be better in the long run if you take the time to figure out your individual pace.

Being inspired by other people is different. Whereas comparison tends to be competitive, being inspired by others allows you to expand your own horizons. You may notice another boxer's agile footwork. Instead of using his skill as a way of putting yourself down— "Look how good he is, I'll never be that good,"—appreciate what it is about his footwork that you like. You might find yourself saying, "He's so light on his feet!" Thus you are inspired to move with a lighter step. When you practice what you see others doing well, you incorporate those same skills into your own routine.

Do not get caught up in "shoulds." Shoulds are part of an inner guilt system. "I shouldn't let myself rest so much. I should work harder." Guilt is one of those emotions that needs to be managed. Bring your mind back to focusing on your BA. "But I really should work harder." Bring your mind back to focusing on BA. This simple act reminds you where your feet are, how to align your hips, torso, and shoulders. Since you have learned all of your techniques in reference to your BA, returning to your Basic Alignment returns you to your workout.

Footwork:
The Slide and Glide

chapter

7

Strength is relaxed power and the ability to let it flow through you.

A boxer's footwork is how she moves around the ring. A boxer practices moving forward, back, and side to side until it becomes instinctual. It is important to maintain the proper width between your feet at all times. Otherwise the base of your stance becomes too narrow, and you could easily lose your balance.

There are two parts to footwork. One is the placement of the feet as the boxer advances, retreats, and moves side to side. You learned how to advance when you learned the step and jab. The basic rule is to lead with the left foot when moving forward, with the right when moving backward; leading with the left foot when going left, and with the right when going to the right. The second part of footwork is the part Muhammad Ali refers to when he says, "Float like a butterfly." Boxers do seem to float. I call it slide and glide. The feet glide across the canvas with just enough friction to make it a slide. It is a smooth, effortless movement, quick and tidy. The slide and glide is an excellent way to condition your legs. A boxer is only as good as his legs are strong. Imagine going ten, twelve rounds constantly moving, ducking, slipping, and punching. Practicing your slide and glide will help develop the strength and coordination you need to box.

Many of us plod through life, often heavy-footed and weighed down by our troubles. When you first try the slide and glide, you might feel like your feet are blocks of wood or cement. This is common. Do not get down on yourself. The difference between a hop and a glide is that a hop comes from an upward lift off of the floor, and a glide is a sliding motion. Hop back and forth a few times, get used to what it feels like to lift up off the floor. Now imagine what it might feel like to move parallel to the floor, to skim the surface. A boxer depends on her ability to move quickly in and out of her opponent's range. This skimming motion, your desired slide and glide, is actually a process of moving your center, or your hips, from one point to another.

Try moving through your center. Moving through your center means your hips move first. Some people incline their heads forward before they move and others shift their shoulders forward. You may put your hands out, or feel tension in your knees before you step. You want to move your center first. Practice your slide and glide in the mirror. Watch for which part of you moves first. Think of your hips gliding parallel to the floor. You use your feet to push back against the floor at the beginning of your glide. If you are maintaining BA (Basic Alignment), the rest of your body will naturally follow when you move through your center. A boxer needs to be concerned about this. If your center is the last part of you to make the shift forward, you will have to waste a second or two getting realigned before you can effectively punch again. Move through your center. That way you always have your punches at your beck and call.

The boxers I have trained often say that the slide and glide hurts their calves. Many people lack muscle tone in the backs of their legs, particularly in the upper thigh. This means that other parts of the legs have to do more than their share of the work. Typically, the quadriceps (quads), the big muscles along the front of the thighs, take on the extra work. But I am having you move from the back of the body forward. So the quads cannot take over. And since the hamstrings, or the backs of the thighs, are not used to working, the calves tend to take the overload. When your calves start hurting, take a moment to stretch them out (see Chapter Eleven). Then resume sliding and gliding, keeping your focus on moving from the center. If you start focusing instead on how you cannot move from your center, switch back to focusing on moving your center, or the hips as a unit, first. It will get easier.

You are never set or tensed, but ready and flexible.
—Bruce Lee, *Tao of Jeet Kune Do*

I worked with a boxer—I'll call her Sylvia—who could not coordinate her slide and glide. She understood that her feet were supposed to move together when she did the slide and glide, with her weight equally distributed between them, but she couldn't actually do it. First she hopped forward with her left, then she slid her right into its correct position. This gave her half a slide but

The time you spend practicing your moves is a chance to perfect your focus, a chance to live your BASIC ALIGNMENT, and a chance to transcend old reactive habits. In this way you will not only learn to box, but you will become the master of yourself.

no glide. It took her a long time of diligent practice to find the proper coordination. Some techniques are harder to grasp than others. I have seen boxers come into the gym who slide and glide without any problem. I practiced the slide and glide for months before I started loosening up. Now my slide and glide is something I do to unwind. One day Sylvia suddenly got it. Out of the blue she went from doing her usual step-step, to a perfect slide and glide. A look of absolute amazement and delight crossed her face. I understand. I have been there. There is nothing like the slide and glide. You literally skim across the floor.

When you watch a good boxer, you will see how the slide and glide is used. A boxer in the gym where I coach was ranked number two in the U.S. in his amateur weight class. He has since turned pro and his boxing skills keep getting better and better. When he was fourteen I remember his skinny legs going back and forth. Now his legs are not so skinny, and his slide and glide is so much who he is that he moves in and out of his opponent's range faster than you can see. He is fluid and powerful, a perfect combination.

Advance and Retreat

STEP 1

Assume BA and then your stance.

Left-handed people will need to reverse their hands and feet from what is shown. Take a few moments to distribute your weight evenly between both feet. Imagine yourself moving through your center, or moving your hips as a unit forward.

Figure 7-1.
Moving through your center, advance. Land on both feet at the same time.

STEP 2

Maintain the same distance between your feet as you move forward six inches.

Move through your center. Both feet land at the same time (see figure 7-1). Be sure you are not landing in a one-two rhythm, with one foot landing and then the other. You want your feet to slide across the floor. Remember you are not lifting up in order to go forward. You are gliding forward through your center.

STEP 3

Move backward, keeping the distance between the feet the same.

It might be a little harder to imagine yourself moving backward through your center (see figure 7-2). Think about the hips, as a unit, moving first. The feet will follow. Again think about gliding across the floor. Do not come up off the floor to get where you are going, but rather move backward in one smooth, gliding motion. If you have a difficult time feeling a smooth motion, keep practicing.

STEP 4

Practice the technique.

Move back and forth, over and over. Each time you move forward you advance into an imagined sparring partner's space, and each time you move backward you retreat from a punch. Stay centered by keeping your weight evenly distributed between your feet. Make sure you are not up on the toes only. If your calves cramp up take a moment to stretch them out.

Figure 7-2.
Retreat, landing on both feet at the same time.

Side to Side

STEP 1

From your stance move to the left, maintaining the same distance between your feet.

Maintaining BA, keeping your feet in their correct stance position, glide to the left about six inches. You are still moving through the center, but this time it is a sideways motion. Both feet land at the same time, with the weight evenly distributed between them.

STEP 2

Move to the right, maintaining the same distance between your feet.

Look at yourself in the mirror. Watch to see if your feet are gliding across the floor. Make sure your hips are level, not one hip up and one down. Also look to see that you are not hopping from place to place. If you are, check to see if you are bending your knees. Your knees should be slightly flexed, not bent.

STEP 3

Practice the technique.

Move side to side, concentrating on landing on both feet at the same time (see figure 7-3). You do not have to move very far. It is more important that you maintain BA, that you keep your feet in their proper stance, and that you feel a rhythm. You may feel clumsy at first, stiff and ungainly. Give your body a chance to get used to it. Remember to be self-aware instead of self-critical.

Figure 7-3.
Move to the side, maintaining the same distance between your feet.

Zig Zag

STEP 1

Assume BA and then your stance. Using the four corners of a square, slide and glide from one corner to another.

The zigzag is a combination of advance, retreat, and side to side with an added diagonal movement. Start at the right rear corner of your imagined square. If you want, draw a square on the floor with chalk or put down tape to show the four corners. Slide and glide in an angle to the left forward corner. Then slide and glide sideways to the right forward corner. Move diagonally to the left rear corner, and finish with a slide and glide to the right rear corner (see figure 7-4). Now you are back where you started!

STEP 2

Practice the technique.

Doing your slide and glide on a zigzag pattern will strengthen all of the major muscle groups in your legs. Do any combination of the four corners, maintaining BA and the same distance between your feet at all times. As you learn to smoothly switch directions, your coordination and balance will improve.

Move through your center and land firmly on both feet. Be careful of your knees during the lateral movement. Make sure that they are slightly flexed.

Remember to remain dynamically tense. You are learning to slip punches and to move in with your punch. You are also practicing being light on your feet.

I learned what an extraordinary length of time three minutes of effort in a ring is; that even holding one's arms extended, especially with the gloves on, requires considerable stamina and strength.
—George Plimpton, *Shadow Box, An Amateur in the Ring*

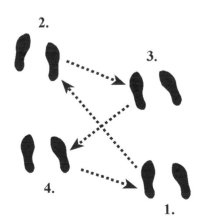

Figure 7-4.
The Zig Zag pattern.

Ask the Coach

I keep losing my balance when I do my slide and glide.

It's possible you are up on your toes. Sink more into your heels and contract your butt muscles to help keep you stable.

I've been trying to distribute my weight more toward my heels, but then I become flat-footed and can't move.

The trick is to feel weight in your heels without actually keeping them on the floor. When you distribute more of your weight toward your heels, they act as a counterbalance, preventing you from tipping forward. Remember to keep your shoulders back and down. This will also keep you from going forward too fast. You are not in a rush to get any-where. Take your time. Learn to slide and glide.

I have done everything you say, and my slide and glide is pretty smooth, but I still feel wooden.

Imagine a sparring partner. When you slide for-ward, you move into your partner's punching zone. This act requires heightened awareness, or dynamic tension. If you have never sparred or play-fought with friends, you might not be able to imagine the risk involved in entering a punching zone. Everyone has something in his life that makes him feel ner-vous or feel at risk. For instance, coming out to your parents if you are gay, asking for a raise, or getting in front of a group of people to perform are all risky activities. As you do your slide and glide, imagine yourself moving in and out of any situation in your life that feels somewhat risky.

Things to Think About

Be considerate of your knees. If you have ever wrenched or strained them, you know how important that is. Even if you have never experienced problems with your knees, it is best to take special care not to strain them. Your knees are joints, and joints are not meant to be stressed, nor are they meant to bear the weight of your movement. Joints are meant to act as hinges. Let your muscles do the work of holding you up.

Stairs can be treacherous. Every step upward can put pressure on your knees. Train yourself to maintain BA when you go up a flight of stairs. Each time you place your foot on the next step, shift your weight to your gluteus (butt) muscle. Think of bringing the force of your step down through the hip and gluteus, and use the hamstring (the back of the thigh) for the power to propel yourself up and forward. Before you step take the time to locate the ninety degree angle made by the gluteus and the hamstring. The act of straightening out the gluteal angle is the force you need to mount stairs without mishap.

Remember, knees and feet go together. Your knees should be lined up over your feet so the kneecap and the toes are going in the same direction. That's why you pivot your foot when you do your hooks. If you didn't pivot your foot, your knee would twist around and end up going in an opposite direction from your foot. This could damage the knee joint by over stretching or possibly tearing ligaments.

Be aware of how you sit. If you tuck your legs under you, it is possible to twist your knees unnecessarily. Sometimes crossing your legs can put pressure on the knee that is underneath. And when you get up from sitting, use your gluteus and hamstring muscles to propel yourself up and out of the chair. A boxer often works out of a crouch when slipping a punch or getting inside her opponent's punches, and the crouch is powered by the gluteal and hamstring muscles. Practice using them whenever you get the chance. Not only will they get stronger, but you will save your knees.

Stretching

Perfecting good form encourages personal precision and clarity of mind.

To stretch is to expand beyond your limits. When you learn to box, your concept of yourself will expand. You will become stronger and more confident as you experience your flexibility and coordination. Partly this happens because of stretching and strengthening your muscles, but it also comes about as your BA (Basic Alignment) becomes a more natural position for you.

Just by assuming BA you have been stretching. There is more to stretching than warming up your muscles before you exercise. When you reach for anything, be it a physical object or a mental goal, you stretch. Successful, rewarding stretching comes from the self-awareness it takes to know that something must change when you feel limited.

Part of what makes stretching an unpleasant experience for some people is that we get distracted by how tight we are. Life can be stressful. If our minds become overloaded and tighten up, our bodies become rigid. We worry and wish we didn't. Our shoulders come up around our ears. Our knees are asked to bear more weight than they are supposed to. Our bellies sag forward, and we try to suck them back in. We run to the gym to work out, run home to eat. But even this is a stretch, for we are expanding our ability to worry and fight our own bodies. Why not stretch toward feeling good?

Stretching becomes a pleasant experience when it is carried out in a comfortable manner. Discomfort around stretching often occurs the moment we feel tight or limited. No one wants to be limited or inflexible. But to start stretching for a goal, you have to begin by feeling tight or limited. Use your stretches as a way of discovering more about yourself. Instead of feeling inflexible and/or angry at how inflexible you are, you can choose to simply be aware of where you are tight.

I worked with a boxer—I'll call him Dennis—who had extremely tight hamstrings. He always had and he had come to accept that he always would. When he assumed BA, he ran into difficulty. He couldn't bring his hips into alignment because his hamstrings were too tight. He insisted he didn't need BA, that he just wanted to box. For a while he did fine by relying on his upper body strength. But one day he came up to me and said he wanted to be more of a fluid boxer. He had been watching boxing on TV and other boxers in the gym. He aspired to be lighter on his feet, to be less stiff and blocky when he punched. I had him focus on assuming his BA. As before, his hamstrings prevented him from comfortably bringing his hips into alignment. Discouraged, he seemed willing to give up, convinced he couldn't do anything about his hamstrings.

Dennis's dilemma is not uncommon. We all have dreams, but attaining them is a different matter. That is why discovery is an important factor. As you do the stretching exercises in this chapter, do them slowly. Instead of being self-critical, get

When fatigue hits, consider you are about to break through to a new level of strength and ability rather than immediately assuming you are tired and can no longer continue.

acquainted with how your body moves. Make a
mental note of where you feel tight. Feeling tight
is not bad. It is how you feel. Once you have
discovered where you feel tight, every time you
encounter that place in a stretch you can switch
your focus to BA. At first it may seem as if nothing is happening, like when Dennis would do the
hamstring stretch. Once he was able to identify
where his muscles were tight, I had him switch his
focus to maintaining BA while in the same position. At first he reported that nothing had
changed. He still felt tight. But when he discovered that focusing on BA made him aware of his
hips, he realized that there was a physical gap
between his hamstring and his hip. He could not

feel his hamstring all the way up to where it connected. This became his new goal, to actually feel the entire hamstring from his knee to where it attached. He would spend ten, fifteen minutes in his hamstring stretch trying to discover more sensation. The sensations he did begin to feel were sensations of release.

Learning to stretch not only helps lengthen and relax overly tight muscles, but also helps you discover the parts of yourself that are overly loose (in other words, flabby). A well balanced body is dynamically tense. I have mentioned dynamic tension before. A toned body has tension that is dynamic or ready to use. A too-tight muscle cannot relax and therefore cannot expand. A flabby muscle cannot tighten and therefore cannot be used. To box you need to be light on your feet, ready to move this way and that, to slip and punch, block and parry. This requires a supple distribution of dynamic tension throughout your body, something you will get better at doing automatically.

The six stretches I cover in this chapter are meant to help you continue discovering the self-awareness that assuming your BA has encouraged. Use these stretching techniques to learn about where you are tight and where you are already loose. Do them at the beginning of a workout to warm up and at any time during a workout or during your day when you feel uncomfortably tight.

Figure 8-1.
The folded leg stretch, front view.

Folded Leg Stretch

STEP 1

Sit on the floor, bend your left leg so the foot comes toward the crotch. Your right leg extends behind you.

Sitting on the floor, shift your weight onto your left butt muscle. Bring your left foot toward your crotch. Remember, everyone's flexibility is different, so your foot may or may not reach your crotch. Your right leg extends behind you (see figure 8-1).

Practice the fundamentals. Return to them again and again. The jab, the hook, the straight right, they are your tools.

STEP 2

Keeping the left butt muscle on the floor, gently press the front of the right hip toward the floor.

This stretch is primarily for the outside of the left hip and upper thigh. To achieve this stretch, make sure you are actually sitting on the left butt muscle, which may or may not tilt your right hip up. With your focus on keeping the left butt muscles on the floor, gently press the front of the right hip (the hip flexor) toward the floor so you will also feel a stretch through the front of the right hip (see figure 8-2). You can push against the floor with your hands to help stabilize you.

Figure 8-2.
The folded leg stretch, pressing the right hip flexor toward the floor.

Keep your upper body erect, with your shoulders in BA position, back and down. Hold the stretch for twenty seconds and relax. Repeat the stretch three times.

STEP 3

Switch legs. Repeat.

When you brush your teeth, rest a leg on the sink and gently stretch your hamstring.

Sitting on the floor, shift your weight to your right butt muscle, bending your right leg so the right foot comes toward your crotch. Your left leg extends behind you. Keeping your right butt muscle on the floor, you want to feel a stretching sensation along the outside of the right hip and upper thigh. Maintaining this position, gently press the left hip flexor toward the floor. Remember to keep your upper body erect, with the shoulders aligned.

STEP 4

Practice the technique.

The hips are an important part of boxing. Your center of gravity is within the pelvic girdle, or hips. Your punches come from power generated by the hips. Either you shift your weight from one side of the hips to the other in preparation for a jab or straight right (reverse this for left-handers), or you whirl your hips into position for a hook. This stretch will help you get in touch with your hips. Take some time with it. Use your hands on the floor to support you while you rock back and forth between the two hips, bringing the butt muscle that is on the floor off the floor. Press it back down into the correct position, paying attention to where you feel tight.

Now work the other side. Press that hip flexor toward the floor, supporting your weight with your arms. Hold your torso very erect. This will stretch the hip flexor. Make sure the leg extending behind you is straight instead of twisted. You want the top of your thigh, not the side of your knee, to be resting on the floor.

Quadriceps Stretch

STEP 1

Holding your left foot with your left hand, pull your foot toward your butt.

While standing take hold of your left foot with your left hand. If it is easier, use a towel or a jump rope around your foot to draw it up toward your butt (see figure 8-3).

STEP 2

Press your left hip flexor forward until your left knee points directly at the floor.

You want to feel this stretch through the hip flexor and quadriceps (see figure 8-4). Sometimes this stretch is done in such a way that the leg bows

Figure 8-3.
Side view of the quadriceps stretch.

Figure 8-4.
Front view of the quadriceps stretch.

back, pulling the hip back. You need to stretch your hip flexors, so make sure your knee points directly at the floor. The side of your body will be straight up and down. If you do not feel a stretch, focus on bringing your hips forward into their BA position. Check to see if your hips are level. Keep the upper body erect, with the shoulders Basically Aligned. If you have trouble keeping your balance, hold onto the wall with your free hand. Hold the stretch for twenty seconds and relax. Repeat the stretch three times.

STEP 3
Switch legs.

Bring your right foot toward your butt with your right hand, using a towel if that's easier. Gently press the right hip flexor forward until the right knee ends up pointing directly at the floor. Make sure the left hip is level with the right hip, and that both hips are in their correct BA position. Maintain the upper body in an erect posture, with the shoulders held in an open position.

STEP 4
Practice the technique.

This is a great stretch for feeling how the hips align. Watch yourself do this stretch in the mirror. When you have one foot drawn up behind you, see what happens when you bow the leg backward. Now assume the correct position, with the knee pointed directly at the floor and the hip flexor of the same leg as flat as possible. Are your hips level? Experiment with them, making them go in opposite directions up and down. Now put them in the correct, level position. Check to see if your shoulders are aligned and if your torso is straight between hips and shoulders. Do you feel a stretch in the quadriceps? If you do not, bring your hips even further forward into alignment.

Hamstring Stretch

STEP 1

From a standing position, place your left foot twelve to eighteen inches in front of you. With both hands above the left knee, gently press down.

With your left foot extended in front of you, place both hands, one on top of the other, just above the left knee. Gently press down until you feel a mild stretch along the back of your left leg (see figure 8-5). It helps if you think of sitting in the air. Your right knee bends, and most of your weight is supported by the right gluteal angle (the angle where the hamstring and gluteal muscles meet). Hold the stretch for twenty seconds and relax. Repeat the stretch three times.

STEP 2

Switch legs.

Position your right foot twelve to eighteen inches in front of you. Placing both hands just above the right knee, gently press down until you feel a stretch along the back of the right leg. Can you feel the stretch all the way from knee to hip? To help facilitate this stretch sit in the air, bending the left knee, using the strength of your left gluteal angle to support you.

STEP 3

Practice the technique.

This is a good stretch. Remember Dennis and his tight hamstrings? He is not alone. Many people are not even aware of their hamstrings. When you do this stretch, the further back you sit in the air, the more aware you will be of the back of your leg. One reason you want access to these long muscles is that they provide essential punching power.

Figure 8-5.
The hamstring stretch.

Triceps Stretch

STEP 1

Standing, bend your left arm and reach down your back as you bring your right arm up behind you. Clasp hands or use a towel to make the connection.

While you are in a standing position, bend your left arm and, holding onto the end of a towel, lower your hand down behind you. Bring your right arm up behind you. Take hold of the towel with your right hand, and gently bring your hands closer together. Stop if you feel pain. Otherwise continue until you are clasping hands (see figure 8-6).

STEP 2

Point your left elbow at the ceiling, square your hips, and straighten the left side of your torso.

Once you have brought your hands as close together behind your back as is comfortable, pay attention to the rest of your body (see figure 8-7). Make sure your feet are aligned pointing forward and your hips are in their BA position. You want your hips level, with the sides of your legs positioned straight up and down. Your shoulders will be open, positioned back and down, and your left elbow will be pointing directly at the ceiling. Make sure both sides of your torso are in a straight line from hip to shoulder. You want to feel this stretch along the underside of the upper arm, your triceps. You will also feel a stretch through the right shoulder. If the stretch is too much, widen the gap between your hands. Your left hand may only be able to reach the top of your back, and your right hand may only be able to reach the lower back. It doesn't matter. Your

Figure 8-6.
Use a towel for the triceps stretch.

stretch will come as you think of bringing your hands together while you maintain the correct position. Hold the stretch for twenty seconds and relax. Repeat the stretch three times.

STEP 3

Switch arms.

While standing bend your right arm behind your head. Bring your right hand down your back to grasp your left hand which is bent behind you and coming up your back. Use a towel to make the connection. If the stretch hurts, widen the gap. Position your body, paying attention to the BA of your feet, the sides of your legs, and your hips. Make sure your shoulders are positioned back and down, and that your right elbow is pointed directly at the ceiling. You want your sides to be in a straight line between hips and shoulders.

STEP 4

Practice the technique.

In this stretch you will have to use the sides of your body (basically your lats) to help you keep the shoulders in their BA position. With both arms behind your back, your shoulders will want to revert to old habits and come forward. The stretch you feel along the underside of the arm that is above your head is the same sensation you will want to feel when you punch. The triceps are extensor muscles; they extend your punches. Many people are not aware of their triceps. I will never forget the day, back when I worked out at the gym where I got my heavy bag, when I was showing off my biceps to a friend. I had worked hard on them, and was proud of the good sized lump they made when I "made a fist." My friend reached over and tapped the underside of my

Figure 8-7.
Maintain BA when doing the triceps stretch.

upper arm, making my flesh jiggle. "Got to work those triceps," she told me. "Biceps aren't anything without the triceps." And she is right; especially when it comes to boxing.

Shoulder Stretch

STEP 1

Maintaining BA, extend your left arm across your chest, cradling it just above the elbow with the right arm.

Assume BA and extend your left arm across your chest (see figure 8-8). Cradle the left arm just above the elbow with your right arm. Check to make sure you have not lost your BA. Do not twist your torso.

STEP 2

Maintaining BA, gently pull your left arm closer to your chest, keeping your hips

Figure 8-8.
The shoulder stretch.

squared forward and your left shoulder in its correct BA position.

Run a mental check on your BA, then gently pull your left arm closer to your chest with your right arm. The left shoulder will want to come forward. Bring it back into alignment. You want your hips squared forward. You will feel a stretch through the left shoulder joint and, if you are holding your torso erect, along both sides of your body. Hold the stretch for twenty seconds and relax. Repeat the stretch three times.

Slow down a little and enjoy yourself.

STEP 3
Switch arms.

Assuming BA, extend your right arm across your chest. Cradle your right arm just above the elbow with your left arm and gently bring your left arm closer to your chest. Make sure your right shoulder stays in its correct BA position, and that your hips remain squared forward.

STEP 4
Practice the technique.

This stretch helps you get used to using your shoulders as joints. Your shoulders are meant to facilitate the movement of your arms. As you do this stretch, concentrate on holding yourself in your BA. Feel your feet on the floor, feel the sides of your legs rising in straight lines to your hips. Keep your hips level and squared forward. Feel them underneath you and feel your sides in a straight line from hips to shoulders. Make sure the shoulder that is being stretched is in its correct BA position. Feel your arms, one crossing in front of your chest, the other acting as a cradle. Think of your head being drawn upwards as if by a string. Your shoulder is like a conduit, a joint through which the energy flows.

Pectoral Stretch

STEP 1

Assuming BA, close your bent arms in front of you until they almost touch.

Assume BA. Bring your arms up in front of you and bend them at the elbows (see figure 8-9). Hold your arms close together with your upper arms parallel to the floor.

STEP 2

Open your arms, keeping your arms bent and your hips squared forward. Close your arms. Repeat.

Maintaining BA, open your arms, keeping them bent (see figure 8-10). You will feel a stretch across the top of your chest. You will get more out of the stretch if you do it slowly, focusing on maintaining your BA through the entire range of motion. Hold the stretch for twenty seconds and relax. Repeat the stretch three times.

Figure 8-9.
Step 1 of the pectoral stretch.

Figure 8-10.
Step 2 of the pectoral stretch.

STEP 3

Practice the technique.

This is a great stretch for getting used to how it feels to use your pecs. Try to maintain "pec consciousness" as you go through everyday life. Do this stretch slowly, opening and closing the arms as if there is resistance to the movement.

Ask the Coach

A friend of mine wanted me to try a stretch she knows about. Should I be careful of what kinds of stretches I try?

Once you have worked with the stretches I have suggested, you will have a better idea of how best to stretch your body. The actual stretch technique is not as important as how you do it.

It's exhausting trying to remember everything.

Yes, and every time you become preoccupied with how hard it is, switch your focus to maintaining your alignment, then return to the exercise.

I didn't understand why stretching is important until I sparred with a woman whose arms are longer than mine by quite a bit. I couldn't get inside to score a point! Finally I kind of flung myself up and over her jab. It worked, except the next day I was so sore I could not get out of bed. Now I stretch all the time. I am amazed at how much longer my reach is.

Now you are understanding relaxed strength.

Things To Think About

Watch boxing when you get the chance. If you have cable you will have plenty of matches to choose from. If you do not have cable, maybe a friend does. Invite yourself over. Check the TV Guide. Wide World of Sports often has boxing matches as part of their program on the weekends. These days there are women's boxing matches on TV as well as men's. When you watch boxing you learn. You may not be able to immediately do what you see, but seeing is an important step toward doing.

You do not have to know all the rules before you can enjoy boxing. You will learn more about the rules as you go along. The basic rules are, you cannot hit below the belt or on the back of the body or head. Points are made for clean punches to the face, chest, and stomach. Boxers are expected to conduct themselves in a respectful manner toward their opponent, the referee, and others who are involved in the match. Clean matches are the ones you will learn the most from. By clean I mean that both boxers work hard to make their points and to defend themselves. They do not make excessive fouls or exhibit sloppy moves. Boxers who train hard and get into the ring to carry out the business of their sport are a joy to watch. They have stamina, their bodies are relaxed and strong, they deliver snappy punches in smooth combinations. When you see boxing of this caliber, you know why it is called a *sweet science.*

You can learn from matches that are not very good. You can learn what not to do. For instance, a boxer may be sloppy in his footwork. He never seems to quite know where his feet are and continually runs into punches because he loses his balance. It may be painful to watch him get beat, but the next time you practice your step and jab, you might be more aware of maintaining your correct foot position. Even if you never plan on getting in the ring yourself, there is a reason for every move you learn. You see the reasons when you watch boxing, and when you train you want to feel as alert as if you were in the ring.

Local boxing gyms usually put on boxing tournaments that you can watch; if they do not, they will be a source of information about local boxing events. Amateur boxers will range in skill from beginners to Olympic level. For the most part amateur boxers are dedicated and serious about their training. Amateur matches have heart and are fun to watch. Professional boxing is a different sport. There is money involved and the boxers do not wear headgear.

Videos with a boxing theme may not have highly original plots, but some are not half bad. Sometimes there is even great boxing footage, though often it is faked. But still, you get to see the drama of it, the handwraps, the gloves, the heavy bag, the hopes and dreams that go along with competitive boxing. They might not be your hopes and dreams exactly, but you can always relate to the basic truths that boxing stories rely on, the truths about finding self in the midst of great travail.

Adding Strength

Practice doesn't make perfect. Focusing on maintaining BASIC ALIGNMENT while practicing your moves will gradually bring you levels of perfection.

Physical strength is the ability to use your muscles. Mental strength is the ability to focus your mind. The combination of mental and physical strength is you. One way to fine tune this combination is to box. I have already talked about the importance of mental focus. One way to sharpen this capability is to bring your awareness back to BA (Basic Alignment) whenever you lose your center. Mental strength is also built by replacing self-critical thoughts with self-aware thoughts.

Physical strength comes through practice. You use your body every day, and the way you use it dictates how your muscles get stronger. It is important to strengthen them from your BA, because then you are strengthening your muscles the way they are meant to work. As you have experienced, assuming BA gives you an immediate boost of strength. And when you box from that alignment, you get even stronger. This chapter provides you with supplementary strengthening techniques that will help you with this process.

The process of getting stronger is a process of shaping yourself. A weight lifter shapes her body

You get what you practice. If you rush through a workout distracted by all sorts of thoughts, you've just strengthened your ability to be distracted.

by the amount of sets and repetitions she does and by how much weight she lifts. The result is a body that is stronger, but her body type would not do well in a boxing ring. Boxers use what is referred to as *relaxed strength*. A boxer's muscles need to be flexible. You want your punches to be fast and powerful. Therefore, you want your strength to be supple and relaxed. A boxer needs a relaxed neck and shoulders; strong arms, especially triceps, that can deliver punch after punch; a torso whose sides, front, and back act as one unit, and whose strength keeps the body erect; flexible hips; gluts and hamstrings that are not only powerful but can work together; and legs and feet that are strong, strong, strong.

Everyone who learns to box starts out by loading up his punches. Loading up means making more show than necessary about punching hard and strong. It is a common reaction. But bunching up the muscles shortens them, and "showing" how strong you are takes more energy than it does to use technique. Technique is always faster and more powerful. You cannot accomplish effective technique with muscles that are not toned. That is why you strengthen them.

Each technique in this chapter targets specific muscle groups and is carried out with the shaping process in mind. For instance, the crunches, punch-ups, and back-ups I have you do all depend on working the shape of the torso as well as targeting the abdomen, obliques, and lower back muscles. Unlike weight lifters, boxers never use a muscle or muscle group all by itself. Each punch, block, or move is a series of steps that flow together. Relaxed strength is knowing which muscles to relax and which to tighten. This constantly shifting balance is what allows a boxer to perform ten to twelve rounds at maximum output. If you already work out at a gym and want to continue doing so, you will want to change your weight training regimen so it supplements your boxing. Lower the amount of weight you lift and raise the number of repetitions. Remember, you do not want your muscles bulky. You want them strong and flexible, coordinated with the rest of your body. Focus primarily on maintaining BA while you go through your repetitions.

I like being around boxers, watching the shaping process happen time after time. When "J.T." first came into the gym wanting to box, he was big and chubby, kind of clumsy and shy. He had never done much in the way of sports, and it took him awhile to find his coordination. Then he started paring down. He got stronger, he stopped slouching. He went from chubby to lean, and his muscle definition started to show. His self-esteem improved. Recently I saw him box in a Golden Gloves Tournament, and though I was glad that he won in his weight class, I was more impressed with how much he had changed. Not only was he confident in the way he moved, but when I congratulated him he looked me right in the eye with a smile, something he had been incapable of doing when he first began.

Another boxer, Casey, started out skinny. Her shoulders hunched forward, she had back problems, and she had very little muscle tone in her

You are the shape of your unconscious intent. As you train and take on the intent of maintaining BASIC ALIGN-MENT, you become the shape of confidence. You become stronger.

arms, legs, or torso. In fact she didn't have a clue how to contact many of her major muscle groups. In spite of this she was determined to box, having been denied opportunities to be active when she was a child Her process was slow at first. She couldn't build muscle that she could not feel. As for shaping herself, she had been an overly skinny, injury-prone person for a long time. It was hard for her to see herself in another way.

If you have never felt your lats, it will be difficult for you to imagine what it is like being able to use them let alone what your body will look like once you do. As long as you strengthen your BA you do not have to worry about what you can or can not imagine. Your muscles, given a chance, will develop in the manner they were meant to. Thus your shape emerges. Prepare to be pleased. Casey is. Now that she maintains her shoulders in an open position, her chest is starting to fill out. Recently she felt her lats when she was working on her house. Soon her torso is going to take on the shape of someone who is no longer overly skinny but lean and muscled.

Scorpion Tail

STEP 1

Kneel on the floor with knees and hands placed shoulder width apart.

This technique works the entire front and back of you, with added benefit to the hips and triceps. Use a mat if kneeling hurts your knees. Take a moment to make sure your hips are parallel to the floor and that your shoulders are open (see figure 9-1).

STEP 2

Tuck your head as you bring your left knee toward your nose.

Keeping your hips parallel to the floor, tuck your head as you bring your left knee up toward your nose (see figure 9-2). It does not matter if your nose and knee touch. Continue to keep your shoulders in an open position and use your triceps to support your upper body.

STEP 3

Extend your left leg back like a scorpion tail as your head bows back as if to meet it. Keep your hips parallel to the floor.

Slowly curve your left leg up behind you as you bring your head back (see figure 9-3). Take a moment to make sure your left hip is not tilted up, but that your hips are level and parallel to the floor. You want to feel a stretch along the front and back of your body on the left side. By keeping the hips parallel to the floor you will work this stretch, thereby strengthening those muscles.

STEP 4

Switch legs.

Repeat the technique, working the right side of the body.

STEP 5

Practice the technique.

Experiment with tilting your hips up and down so you know what it feels like to

Figure 9-1.
Keep your back straight, do not let it go swaybacked.

Figure 9-2.
Tuck your head toward your knee.

Figure 9-3.
The scorpion tail.

keep them level and parallel to the floor. You may want to look at yourself in the mirror. Also experiment with bringing your shoulders up around your ears so you know what that feels like. Now bring them back into an opened position. This opens up your chest. As you repeat the scorpion tail, slow it down. Think about working your body. The more you keep your hips from moving, the more of a workout you will get. If you are ready for more resistance, put a leg weight around your ankle. Do three sets of ten repetitions each to begin with. If this is too difficult, reduce the number of repetitions. If it doesn't challenge you, slow down the technique to make sure you have the correct form before adding more reps.

Crunches (Abdominal)

STEP 1

Lie on your back with your knees up and your feet flat on the floor. Touch your fingertips to the side of your head with your elbows extended to either side.

This technique primarily works the abdominal muscles, with added benefit to the sides of your torso and your lower back. Lying on your back, hold your arms at either side of your head with fingertips touching and elbows extended (see figure 9-4).

STEP 2

Maintain your focus on lifting through the sides of the body. Bring the torso as a unit up off the floor keeping the lower back pressed to the floor.

Slowly bring your torso off the floor three to five inches. Think of lifting yourself up with the rods that go along the side of your body. Keep your lower back pressed to the floor (see figure 9-5). Keeping your lower back pressed to the floor will prevent you from coming very far off the floor; this will help work your entire torso. Also it is very important to keep the neck straight and relaxed, in line with the torso. You do not want to come up off the floor by bending your neck and lifting with your head. Do not forget to breathe.

STEP 3

Lower your torso without touching your head to the floor. Repeat.

Continue through all of your repetitions without touching your head to the floor. Bring your torso up by lifting with the sides of your body and keeping the lower back to the floor. Keep your neck straight, in line with your body. You will feel this in the abs as well as in the rest of your torso.

STEP 4

Practice the technique.

Feel your feet on the floor. Feel your lower back pressing against the floor. Feel the way your legs bend, how they connect to your feet and hips. Feel those rods along the sides of your torso, picture them connecting your hips and your shoulders. With your neck parallel to the floor, lift

Figure 9-4.
Keep your neck straight.

Figure 9-5.
Keep your lower back pressed to the floor.

up a few inches, just enough to feel your abdomen contract deep inside. This technique works the muscles from the inside of the belly out. You will also be working the sides of your torso and your lower back. You do not want to push your belly out. You can prevent this from happening by keeping your lower back pressed to the floor. To begin, do three sets of ten to fifteen repetitions each. If it is too much, do less. If you cannot feel that you have worked your abs, make sure your form is correct before adding more reps.

Punch–Ups (Abdominal and Obliques)

STEP 1

Lie on the floor in the same position as you did for crunches, except hold your arms in the on guard position.

This technique primarily works your abs and obliques with added benefit to the sides of your torso and your lower back. Lie down with your knees bent and your feet flat on the floor. Take your on guard position with your fists on either side of your face (see figure 9-6).

STEP 2

Keeping your lower back flat to the floor, lift up three to five inches and stop. Holding your position, slowly punch right and then left.

Keeping your lower back pressed to the floor, lift up three to five inches using

Figure 9-6.
Neck in a straight line, lower back pressed to the floor, shoulders down.

your imaginary side rods. Hold your position. Punch with the right hand (see figure 9-7). As your right arm returns on the same plane to its correct position, punch with your left hand.

STEP 3

After two punches lower your torso toward the floor without touching your head to the floor. Repeat.

Your form is important while doing punch-ups. You want to feel your torso as one unit rising up off the floor, as one unit holding you off the floor as you punch right and punch left, then as a unit lowering you toward the floor. But your head doesn't get to rest. Keep your neck from bending as you go up and down. The slower you go, the better the workout will be.

STEP 4

Practice the technique.

Punch-ups are different from crunches. The action of holding yourself in the air while you punch takes energy. Focus on maintaining excellent form and on making clean, precise punches. It is the act of punching that uses your oblique muscles, the muscles that connect the front of you to the back of you over the tops of your ribs. Keep your lower back pressed to the floor. Lift up with your entire torso, making sure your neck is not bent forward. And fill those punches with intent. Punch slow but hard. To begin with do three sets of ten to fifteen repetitions each. If it is too much, reduce the reps. If you cannot feel your abs and obliques working, make sure your form is correct before adding more reps.

Figure 9-7.
Keeping your lower back pressed to the floor, punch right and left.

Back-ups

STEP 1

Lie on your stomach with your fingertips touching the sides of your head, your elbows extended to either side.

This technique primarily works the muscles of your lower back and gluts, with added benefit to the rest of your torso. Lying on your stomach, bring your arms up so your elbows extend to either side with your fingertips touching the sides of your head (see figure 9-8).

STEP 2

Keeping your hips on the floor, lift up three to five inches using your imaginary side rods.

Keeping your hips on the floor, looking straight in front of you and with a straight neck, lift up three to five inches. Use those imaginary side rods to lift yourself (see figure 9-9). It is important to imagine the side rods and to experience your torso as a unit. You do not want to sway the lower back, but to lift up as one solid unit.

Figure 9-8.
Step 1 of back-ups.

STEP 3

Repeat.

Your arms extending out to either side will help you keep your chest open and your shoulders down in the correct BA position. Each time you lower toward the floor, do not completely relax, but continue slowly lifting and lowering until you have completed your repetitions.

Figure 9-9.
Step 2 of back-ups.

STEP 4

Practice the technique.

This technique is to be done gently and slowly. If there is any pain in your lower back, do not lift up off the floor so far. The most important part is maintaining your torso as a unit. Lift through those side rods. Keep your hips on the floor. Look straight in front of you and keep your neck straight. To begin with do three sets of ten repetitions each. If your lower back hurts, reduce the number of reps and correct your form. If you cannot feel your lower back working, make sure your form is correct before adding more reps.

Leg Lift (Outside of Thigh)

STEP 1

Lie on your left side with your legs under a chair. Raise your right leg from the hip approximately twelve inches.

This technique primarily works the muscles on the outside of your upper thigh and hip with added benefit to your torso. Slowly raise your right leg from the hip approximately twelve inches, or until your leg meets the chair (see figure 9-10).

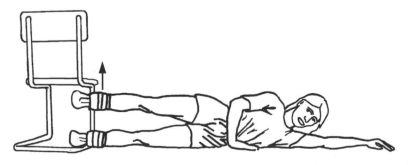

Figure 9-10.
Keep your body in a straight line.

STEP 2

Lower your right leg without resting it. Repeat.

Raise and lower your leg without resting in between until you have completed all of your repetitions. Remember to maintain your BA. Even though you are lying on your side, you want your body aligned in a straight line. Use your right hand to help stabilize you.

STEP 3

Switch legs.

STEP 4

Practice the technique.

The reason you are doing this technique is to strengthen the outside of your thighs from hip to knee. This will come about the more you focus on maintaining your BA. The common tendency is to fall over. Use your hand on the floor to keep you in place. If you desire more resistance, use leg weights. To begin with do three sets of ten to fifteen repetitions each. If your leg hurts reduce the amount of reps. If you cannot feel the muscles on the outside of your thigh and hip working, make sure you have the correct form before adding more reps.

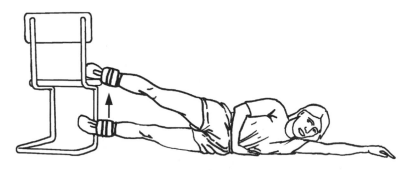

Figure 9-11.
Raise your leg slowly.

Leg Lift (Inside of Thigh)

STEP 1

Lie on your left side with your right leg resting on top of a chair. Slowly raise the left leg approximately twelve inches.

This technique primarily works the inside of the thigh with added benefit to your torso. Lie on your left side. Rest your right leg on top of a chair. Lift your left leg approximately twelve inches, remembering to maintain BA (see figure 9-11).

STEP 2

Lower your left leg without resting it. Repeat.

Slowly lower your leg. The slower the better. Do not rest it, but continue with your repetitions. Make sure your body is lined up. Really work that leg. Take your time to feel the muscles along the inside of your thighs from your groin to your knee.

STEP 3
Switch legs.

STEP 4
Practice the technique.

Experiment with putting and keeping your body in a straight line. This in itself can be a good workout. Boxers depend on little shifts of the body for their precision. These movements may seem like nothing, but they require immense control. Such control comes from working the little muscles as well as the bigger ones. To begin with do three sets of ten to fifteen repetitions. If your leg hurts reduce the reps. If you cannot feel the inside of your thigh working, make sure you have the correct form before adding more reps.

Triceps Extension

STEP 1

Holding a dumbbell in your left hand, bend over so your back is parallel to the floor and your left arm is bent at a ninety degree angle.

This technique primarily works your triceps with added benefit to your torso and legs. Bend over holding a dumbbell in your left hand. Make sure your back is parallel to the floor and that your left arm is bent at a ninety degree angle (see figure 9-12). Check to see if you have the correct position by looking in the mirror. Rest your right hand on a chair to help keep your balance.

STEP 2

Keeping your left elbow stationary, extend the dumbbell behind you until your entire arm is parallel to the floor.

It is important to keep your elbow stationary as you extend the dumbbell behind you until your entire arm is parallel to the floor (see figure 9-13). Continue to keep your back parallel to the floor, and make sure you do not extend your arm above your back.

Figure 9-12.
Keep your lower back parallel to the floor.

Figure 9-13.
Do not bring your arm above your back.

STEP 3

Return your arm to its original position. Repeat.

Continuing to maintain your back parallel to the floor, return your left arm to its original ninety degree angle. Use your right hand on the chair to help you keep your balance.

STEP 4

Switch arms.

Follow the same steps with the right arm.

STEP 5

Practice the Technique.

You want to feel the back of your upper arm working. Make sure your back is parallel to the floor and take the time to check out your hips. You want your hips in their BA position, level with one another and positioned directly over the feet. Make sure your shoulders are also in their BA position. You want your chest to be open, and you want your torso supported by the imaginary rods that go down each side. These side rods will tell you when your back is parallel to the floor. As you extend the dumbbell, keep that elbow stationary. Continue to hold it stationary while you lower your arm and continue on through your repetitions. To begin with do three sets of ten repetitions each. If your triceps cannot take it, reduce the reps. If you cannot feel your triceps working, make sure you have the correct form before adding more reps.

Ask the Coach

My lower back hurts when I do my crunches.

You could be coming up too far off the floor. This isn't a contest, isn't a sit-up, it's a crunch. More important than anything else is that you focus on lifting your torso as a unit, using those imaginary rods that run along the sides of your upper body as stabilizers. Your abdominal muscles basically connect those imaginary rods, so by lifting up through the imaginary rods you will automatically be using your abs as well as learning to use your torso as one unit.

At first I thought the scorpion tail didn't do anything. Then I slowed it down like you said, and the next day I was sore all through my stomach and down my back. It's a great technique.

It is. Basically it puts you in the same position that a powerful punch does. Those muscles you feel are the ones you will use to punch at the full extent of your range.

I had a car accident the other day. I was rear ended, but would you believe it, I didn't suffer any injury? Without thinking about it my body automatically assumed my punch-up position, and instead of my neck getting whiplash, my torso moved forward as a unit. All those crunches and punch-ups have really paid off. Not only am I getting good at boxing, but I'm a lot safer for being aligned and stronger.

Realizing you can take care of yourself in crisis and that you can trust your own strength and instincts is worth ten trophies. Good for you.

Things to Think About

How do you see yourself? Timid? Confident? Do you consider yourself coordinated or awkward? Are you a lucky person or an unlucky person? What kind of weight do you carry on your frame? Does this make you a big, medium, or small person? I have seen all kinds of people come into the gym, from painfully awkward to suave, from six to sixty-five. It does not matter. Everyone can box. The point is, you will start boxing as who you think you are and through boxing you will become who you really are.

How would you like to be? Stronger in mind and body? Leaner? More aggressive? Less fearful? Better coordinated? More flexible? A Golden Gloves champ? Everyone has a goal and all goals are attainable. You have to put in the effort to reach them, but being the kind of person you want to be is well worth some effort. As you work out remember to keep in mind the changes you would like to see in yourself. Do not be shy about imagining them. Believe in yourself.

Think of power flowing through your arms. The power comes from your center. When your body is aligned, power can flow without kinks or detours right out your closed fist through the punching bag. Bam! Muhammad Ali says his punch takes less than a fourth of a second to make its claim. That is fast. It is an example of power. Power comes when you get out of your own way. Let self-criticism and emotional reaction go by the wayside. They just get in the way.

Allowing your power to flow through you will shape your body. Repetitive movement will burn off excess fat and tone your muscles. As you feel stronger you hold yourself with more confidence. Confidence encourages you to work a little harder, and the stronger you are the more power you can exert. You will begin to understand how power does not come from the body alone. This understanding will have you throwing your punches more from your center. The more you do this the more you work all the little muscles deep within you. This carves away more excess fat and tightens your muscles into elastic bands. Your body acquires muscle definition which, being visible to the eyes, encourages you to see yourself as strong. More and more you use this strength for everyday things like sitting, lifting, and walking. Other people perceive you as strong and vital. You accept this as your self image, and in the gym you sharpen your discipline to perfect this newfound power. The process goes on and on, shaping you, bringing you closer and closer to yourself.

Getting a Workout

chapter

10

During your minute rest period in between rounds practice clearing your mind of any thoughts. Worrying or thinking tends to impose tension on the body.

A workout is an amount of time set aside for you to practice attaining your goals. In this case your goal is learning to box. There are a number of factors that influence a workout:

- The level of boxing at which you want to participate

- The amount of time you wish to spend on each workout

- Whether you are self-motivated or group-motivated

- The quality of the time you spend working out

- Your emotional/mental and physical state at the time of the workout

- How the workout fits into your long range goals

I will discuss each of these factors to help you decide what kind of workout is the best for you. Your workouts will become a kind of backbone to your life. Not only will they help keep you toned and trim, but they will be a source of energy. You

The business of competition is partly the ability to put on a good show of honest endeavor and good technique. Winning is nice, too.

will come to depend upon them as a way of releasing stress and toxins, and as a way of enhancing your own personal vitality.

What are your boxing goals? Do you want to compete? The competitive levels of boxing are professional and amateur. Depending on what kind of shape you are in to begin with, you can expect to train nine to twelve months or more before you are ready for your first match. You can train at a competitive level without competing. Recreational boxers have a choice of sparring or not. The majority of recreational boxers do end up sparring at least once. The boxing fitness level is geared toward people who want to get in shape.

Deciding what level of boxing you want to start at depends on what kind of time you have. If you lead a busy life your workouts have to fit into that schedule. Be honest with yourself. What kind of time do you have to set aside for working out? Set a workout routine you can stick to. Try to include two to three workouts a week for getting in shape. Competitive boxers work out one to two hours three times a week to begin with. I recommend recreational boxers do the same.

Once you have decided what kind of time you have to devote to boxing, take another honest look at yourself. Are you the inner-motivated type or an outer-motivated type? Discipline is part of working out. It is a fact of life that we have to follow rules to get where we are going. Sometimes we have to buckle down and do what is in front of us, which takes discipline. Discipline is the authority that makes sure we accomplish what we set out to do. It can either be an inner authority, self-imposed, or an outer authority that is set by a coach or trainer. If you are good at motivating yourself, working out alone will not be a problem for you. You can get a bag and start right in. If you prefer working out with others, either join a gym or a boxing fitness type program. Organize a group of friends who will commit to a workout routine with you. If you want to compete, whether you are self-motivated or not, get a coach.

Coming to each workout fresh is not always easy. Your workouts will probably be crammed into your life. Professional boxers are different: boxing is their job, that is what they do. The rest of us fit boxing into our lives. For your workout to be an energizing force in your life you have to know how to use that time to its maximum. Shedding your everyday self and becoming your workout self is a good time to switch over your mental process. Put aside mental worries as you change clothes. The mental process is like a muscle; it gets stronger through practice. As you prepare to work out, put each distracting thought that comes through your mind aside, automatically checking in with your BA (Basic Alignment) instead. This helps you get into your body. By the time you are wrapping your hands and putting on your gloves, you will be in boxing mode.

Training is the map of how you come to understand your own talents and strengths through persistence and self-awareness.

In boxing mode your mind serves you. But you have to train your mind to serve. Otherwise it will

If you are tense you lose energy.

continue on its cluttered, worrisome way, distracting you from your purpose. Your purpose is to have a good workout. Yet you come to each workout in a different state of mind, ranging from tired and depressed to energetic. You will learn to check your emotional reactions (I am tired, I cannot go on, this is too hard, etc.) by focusing on BA instead. This is a big job. Be patient with yourself. You are your mind and your body; it takes time to bring them together into a cohesive whole. That is what your workouts are for–to meld your mind and body into one. Stick with it, for it is worth it.

It doesn't always feel simple. Some workouts are harder than others. In a moment of feeling puny or tired you might want to quit. Finish with your workout before you decide. It is focus that gets you through a challenging workout. I will talk more about different focuses you can choose from later on in this chapter. But get through your workout. You may want to slow it down, or do less than previously planned, but try not to give up on yourself. After the workout is over, remind yourself that one workout is just one step in the bigger plan. One step, or even a series of steps, may be hard but it will not always be like that. Training is a rhythmical process. There are ups and downs. Taking it all in stride is one of the ultimate goals. A boxer must be prepared to meet unexpected challenges. All he has to rely on is his training. It is the same thing in everyday life. When it comes down to it, you have to depend on yourself. So when the going gets a little rough, do not give up.

In the boxing gym everyone's workout is regulated by the same timer, generally set for a three minute round with a thirty second bell that tells you to go all out. The working round is followed by a one minute rest period. The workout routines I have listed in this chapter are based on a number of rounds for each technique. You can use any kind of timer except a clock. You end up watching the clock instead of focusing on the technique you are learning. You can also work out to songs that are a specific length. Your rounds do not have to be three minutes. Depending on age and experience, boxers will box either one, two, or three minute rounds. The whole point of doing rounds is that you maintain your chosen focus from beginning to end. That is how you develop mental toughness and the ability to go on beyond your own limits.

Your boxing training will put you in the best shape of your life. The rewards are endless. Treat your workouts with respect. They will serve you best when you take them seriously. Find out what you are capable of. Most important, have fun.

Workout 1: No Equipment

Workout 1 runs approximately one hour. I recommend you do it three times a week. It does not require any equipment. The rounds can be one, two, or three minutes each. Remember to take a one minute resting round between each working round. During the one minute resting round remain in a dynamically ready frame of mind. If you are winded, use this time to slow down your breathing. If distracting thoughts crowd your head, use this time to put them aside and maintain BA instead.

I have suggested a focus for each of these rounds. Following each round description, I list other focus options. Your focus is important. A three minute round can feel like a long time. If it does, keeping your mind on your focus will get you through with self-awareness. Having a specific focus also helps you pinpoint what aspect of the technique you wish to work on. At first it is impossible to keep track of all the details that go into a perfected skill. Eventually you will put all the details together naturally.

Keep a record of your workouts (see tables 10-1 and 10-2). Put down exactly what you did during each workout and jot down notes of what you did and didn't feel. Keep track of any changes you are conscious of. Consider this workout sheet a map of where you have been. You are charting your way into unknown territory: namely you. You might think some small detail is insignificant, but put it down. You could be confused by a technique and not know it. If you write it down, eventually you will get the message: you are confused. Review the chapter covering the technique you are confused about. Each time you read about a technique, a detail that you had missed will leap off the page at you. With that new focus in mind, you can return to your workouts renewed.

STEP 1

Warm up: Stretch for ten to fifteen minutes.

Read Chapter Seven on stretching. Go through each of the stretches slowly, keeping the manual close by for easy reference. The point in stretching is to discover where you are tight and where you lack muscle tone. Both areas need to be stretched. When you experience discomfort from a stretch, hold the position for a moment and breathe deeply until you feel ready to go on. If at any time you feel pain, you could be pushing the stretch too far. Back off the stretch until the pain diminishes.

STEP 2

One round in stance, maintaining BA.
Focus: self-awareness instead of self-criticism.

This round is harder than you might think. Watch yourself in a mirror. Take your stance and maintain BA. Throughout the round continually assume BA, trying to feel the position of your feet, hips and shoulders, and trying to feel your torso as a unit. Remember, the focus is self-awareness. That means you are trying to see how your body shifts into BA, or you are trying to feel how your body shifts into BA.

Focus Options: Put hips in and out of alignment. Open and close the shoulders. Bring the torso forward as a unit over the hips.

STEP 3

One round footwork, advance and retreat.
Focus: maintaining BA.

In this round you will maintain whatever BA you were able to tap in the previous round while doing your advance and retreat footwork. Refer to Chapter Five to read about footwork.

Focus Options: Move purposefully in and out of opponent's space. Keep hips level and parallel to the floor. Use imaginary side rods to hold your torso erect.

STEP 4

One round footwork, side to side.
Focus: slide and glide.

Switch to the side to side technique, focusing on trying to slide and glide. It is important to discover

**The Four C's of
Amateur Boxing:**
If you are coachable, in
condition, and concentrate
on your boxing, you will be a
champion.
— John Brown, *The Boxing
Manual*

the slide and glide. If you do not feel it you will continue working toward that goal in subsequent workouts, and if you do feel it, you will work toward feeling it more consistently.

Focus options: Place the feet, landing with equal weight on both. Keep the hips in correct alignment, making sure they do not sway or tilt. Evade punches.

STEP 5

One round footwork, zigzag.
Focus: moving through the hips.

Before you start this round decide on the zigzag pattern you will be doing. Your focus is moving through the hips. Refresh your memory on what that means by referring to Chapter Five. Concentrate. This focus is important. Remember, you may come out of the round feeling you still do not know what it is to move through the center. It is something to continue working toward.

Focus Options: Slide and glide. Maintain the body as one unit. Keep the shoulders back and down.

STEP 6

One round jab.
Focus: maintaining BA.

Review the jab in Chapter Three. In order to jab from your center rather than your shoulder, you need to practice. That is why you will focus on maintaining BA in this round. Maintaining BA brings your awareness to being lined up and aware of your hips, to keeping your shoulders back and down. Still, this round will tire out your shoulder. Slow the punch down when this happens, and keep reverting your focus to maintaining BA. It will help keep your mind off the fact that you are tired.

Focus Options: Light, quick jabs. Two hard jabs, one light; repeat. Technique.

STEP 7

One round straight right.
Focus: pushing back against the floor through the rear foot.

Review this punch. Use this round to find a connection between the rear foot pushing back against the floor and the power of your punch. In a mirror watch to see that your rear foot is lined up correctly. If you do not have a mirror, every once in a while turn and look down at your rear foot to see if it is lined up.

Focus Options: Power. Keep your shoulders back and down. Feel the imaginary side rods.

STEP 8

Two rounds step and jab.
Focus: correct technique.

Review the step and jab in Chapter Three. Remember, self-awareness instead of self-criticism. Do not come down on yourself for not getting the technique correctly, just keep bringing your awareness to getting the feel of the technique. Every little move will need to be monitored at first. Get on yourself to maintain your BA in the background as you go through all the moves laid out in Chapter Three. Two rounds on this one.

Focus Options: Keep the hips and shoulders lined up. Power. Move through the hips, or center.

STEP 9

Two rounds footwork, advance and retreat, side to side and zigzag.
Focus: keeping your hands up in their correct position.

Have you noticed that it is difficult to keep your hands up at all times? The strength to do this primarily comes from your torso. Continually remember to keep your shoulders back and down so you cannot keep your arms up by your shoulders alone. These two rounds you will be utilizing all three slide and glide moves, but the main focus is on keeping your hands up. Go for it.

Focus Options: Move precisely from place to place. Feel the slide and glide. Bring your weight down through your heels.

STEP 10

Ten to fifteen minutes strengthening techniques.

Start out with three sets of each technique. Review Chapter Eight for the recommended amount of repetitions.

STEP 11

Practice the technique.

How did it go? Did you record what you did? Also put down anything that occurred to you while you were working out (things you weren't sure about, what you liked, what you discovered). Did you remember to put the one minute rest round in between the working rounds? Did you stay dynamically alert during the rest round? Were you able to keep your mind on your chosen focus? How is this length of a workout for you? Was it too hard, not hard enough? I have outlined other workouts for you to choose from, or you can put together one of your own now that you have an idea of what does and does not work for you. Make sure your workouts are a balance of hard and fun. You want to push yourself to get better, but you want to have fun, too. You want to come away from a workout feeling energized. It is good to have your muscles pleasantly sore. It can even be helpful because then you feel them. But you do not want a workout to wipe you out. If that is how you feel, cut back the amount of rounds you are doing.

Workout 2: With Equipment

Workout 2 runs about an hour, but is a more intense workout than Workout 1. You will be going ten rounds, two or three minutes each with a one minute rest in between. Again, I have suggested a focus for each round and have added focus options at the end of each round description. Remember to have the manual handy so you can refer to it.

STEP 1

Warm up: stretch for ten to fifteen minutes.

Do each stretch listed in Chapter Seven, concentrating on feeling where your muscles are tight, where they are not toned. See how much range you can get out of each stretch. You get more range when you take the stretch to the edge of discomfort, pause to breathe deeply, then gently push into the stretch until the discomfort rises a notch or two. Pause, hold, and breathe before letting up.

STEP 2

Two rounds jump rope.
Focus: bringing your weight gently down through your heels.

Review Chapter Six on skipping rope. Every time you get tired try to last a few more rotations of the rope by concentrating on your focus, bringing your weight down through your heels. By the end of the first round you want to know if you land more on the balls of your feet or on your heels. Make appropriate corrections. If you get too tired to go on, swing the rope from side to side, continuing to focus on bringing your weight down through your heels.

Focus Options: Maintain BA, especially in the shoulders. Keep the rope going two more rotations longer than you did the time before. Perfect the two-footed step.

STEP 3

Two rounds step and jab.
Focus: keeping chest open, torso erect.

Feel a little spring in your step. Remember, you are advancing into an opponent's space. Stay alert, keep your intent moving forward. Push back through the rear foot, and move smoothly across the floor.

Focus Options: Bring your weight down more through your heels than the balls of your feet. Keep your punch on the same plane when it is delivered and when it is returned. Keep your hips squared forward.

STEP 4

Two rounds jab and straight right.
Focus: shifting your weight correctly.

Do these rounds either on the heavy bag or shadowboxing. Review Chapter Four on punching to make sure you are doing the weight shift correctly. Your entire focus is on getting a feel for that weight shift before each punch. Remember to vary your rhythm so you do not get bored. Punch one-two, or, one, one-two, or, one-pause-two, etc.

STEP 5

One round footwork, advance and retreat, side to side and zigzag.
Focus: feeling the slide and glide.

Go over your BA before you start so you can maintain it without it being the major focus. Now go for that slide and glide. Move through the center. Think of gliding from spot to spot on the floor. Do not come down on yourself if you feel clunky instead. Bring your focus back to wanting to feel the slide and glide, even if just for a fleeting moment. Quickly reevaluate your BA then bring your mind back to the slide and glide.

Focus Options: Keep the shoulders back and down. Keep your hands up. Slip punches each time you move.

STEP 6

Three rounds on the heavy bag.
Focus: keeping the wrists straight and maintaining correct technique.

Refer to Chapter Four on punching a heavy bag. Keep those wrists straight! Get your weight behind your punches. Distinguish between straight punches and hooks. Use the same focus for each round or have a different focus each time.

Focus Options: Perfect straight punch technique. Perfect hook technique. Maintain BA.

STEP 7

Ten to fifteen minutes strengthening technique.

Work your torso. Do your crunches, punch-ups, back-ups, and the scorpion tail slowly and with fierce concentration. Feel your lower back on the floor, keep your neck in line with your torso, carry out each repetition with the intention to shape your body into a powerful unit. Build those triceps, and inner and outer thighs, knowing that the better toned your muscles are the stronger your punches will be.

STEP 8

Practice the technique.

Pay attention to your feet. You do not want to be up on the balls of your feet. During your footwork rounds is a good time to note where on your feet you do land. If your feet are turned out or in, you can gently correct this each time you slide and glide from one place to another. When you are skipping rope is a good time to really monitor your BA. Even if it isn't your main focus, quickly check from time to time to make sure your shoulders are back and down, your chest is open, and that your hips are directly under your shoulders. Remember the greater picture. This is boxing. If you get too caught up in getting all the details right, do some rounds in which you focus on boxing. Advancing into someone's space is risky; retreating is not a defensive move, but is about holding your own. Side to side is a quick, elusive move, and the zigzag takes great skill. Do your footwork with meaning. Punch with meaning. Jab hard, jab light, jab from far away, jab in close. The point of boxing is to have an effect, to make points, and to know your own capabilities.

Workout 3: Getting Serious

This workout runs approximately one and one-half hours. I recommend you do it three times a week. Try to keep your energy level up throughout the workout. That means during the resting rounds you are quiet and ready, not collapsed. Use the resting rounds to calm your breathing; when the bell sounds go into the next round determined to work as hard as you can. If you get tired keep your mind on your chosen focus. Quiet your breathing. One way to do this is by taking deep, slow breaths from the belly. Try to breathe through your nose. This will encourage you to breathe deeper.

STEP 1

Warm up: stretching ten to fifteen minutes.

Use the stretching techniques covered in Chapter Seven to help you access your BA. You have to work the techniques, which means assuming the correct position, then applying consistent and gentle pressure to stretch and feel more and more of your body. Look at your body, how your feet attach to your legs, your legs to your hips, how your torso rises up from your hips and gluts, and how your shoulders are a framework from which your arms hang. I know there is extra flesh here and there, and that you may not even be able to feel how your body goes together. That is what stretching is for. Stretching helps you put yourself together so you can box.

STEP 2

Three rounds skipping rope.
Focus: BA.

There is maintaining BA, and there is tightening your BA. Tightening it is analogous to tightening a nut and bolt so you have an increasingly solid structure. Skipping rope is a good time to tighten your BA. You do this by continually focusing on trying to feel that your feet, hips, and shoulders are lined up, and that your torso is a unit that holds you up. Eventually you will feel the muscled shape of your hips and you will be able to use them to get more out of your boxing. You will feel your lats contracting and relaxing; you will be toned inside and out.

Focus Options: Bring your weight down through the heels. Use your lats to turn the rope. Relax your neck.

STEP 3

Two rounds step and jab.
Focus: intent.

When you step and jab, mean it. That does not mean rush it; do not lean forward off your center. Review Chapter Three for punching tips. Perfect your technique, but focus on having every inch of your body behind that step and jab. You do this by getting all of you aligned, stretched, and strengthened and by filling up these rounds with intent. You are stepping into an opponent's space with a punch. You mean business.

Focus Options: Place your feet correctly. Keep the hips correctly aligned.

STEP 4

Two rounds footwork, advance and retreat, side to side, and zigzag.
Focus: maintain BA and slide and glide.

Focus Options: Try to feel what it is like to move your center (hips) first, letting the rest of the body follow. Feel a rhythm (work out to music). Try to feel your body move as one unit.

STEP 5

Two rounds jab and straight right on heavy bag.
Focus: technique.

Working your technique does not necessarily mean punching hard. Review Chapter Three and go over in your head the series of details that create your straight punches. Practice the sequence of these details until they become a pattern that feels natural to you.

Focus Options: Gut level punching. (Keep those wrists straight!) Change the rhythm (one-two, one, one-two, one-two, two, etc.). Keep the shoulders back and down, punching from the lats.

STEP 6

Two rounds hooks on heavy bag.
Focus: technique.

Review Chapter Three. Establish in your mind the details that make up your hooks. Practice each detail and then read the chapter again, looking for any detail you might have missed or misinterpreted. Practice the details in their correct sequence until a pattern emerges that makes sense to you. Take time with your hooks. Think about the direction of the force that is behind your hooks. If you cannot feel your hooks coming from your body, refer to Chapter Eight on how to do the scorpion tail. This technique works the entire length of your body, front and back. Do crunches, punch-ups, and back-ups to help build up your torso. Strengthen your triceps, the inside and outside of your thighs. In other words, build your hooks, work hard at getting them to work for you.

Focus Options: Gut level punching. (Pay extra attention to keeping your wrists straight.) Maintain BA. Correctly pivot the feet.

STEP 7

**Two rounds mixed punches on heavy bag.
Focus: gut level punching.**

Mix your punches up. Do them in different combinations. Vary their impact. Make some of them hard, some of them light and snappy, hard and snappy, etc. Have fun and get into it.

Focus Options: Correct position of the feet. Correct weight shifts. Keep the hips forward under the shoulders and over the feet.

STEP 8

**Two rounds footwork, side to side, jabbing each time you land in a new position.
Focus: technique.**

Review the appropriate chapters so you feel clear about how to do your side to side and your jab. Now put them together. Each time you land to one side or the other you jab. You may want to slow your slide and glide down until you get the rhythm of this combination. Now your slide and glide means you are moving to the side smoothly and quickly so you can fire off a jab, then moving to the other side so you can fire off another jab, etc.

Focus Options: Move your hips first. Distribute your weight evenly to all parts of your feet. Keep the shoulders back and down.

STEP 9

**Two rounds speed bag.
Focus: technique.**

Review Chapter Five on speed bag technique. Work one hand at a time, then alternate them. As you get the rhythm pick up the pace.

Focus Options: Maintain BA. Use your lats to hold your hands up. Shift your weight back and forth between your feet.

STEP 10
Fifteen minutes strengthening techniques.

Explore the techniques laid out for you in Chapter Eight. Slow them down until you understand exactly how they work for you. Then work the techniques and build your muscle tone, pare away excess fat, and shape your body so you can use it to put more power into your punches.

STEP 11
Practice the technique.

After your workout, take the time to write down everything you did. Think back over the workout and jot down anything you remember. For instance, if suddenly you start stepping on your jump rope when you had not before, you might be inclined to be impatient with yourself. You might get irritated that you messed up. But if you simply note it on your workout sheets, you will be more aware that a new pattern is occurring. When you take the time to pay more attention to what is going on, it becomes clear that in the process of tightening your BA, your left foot has tended to wander more to the side. Once you correct the position of your left foot, you stop stepping on the rope.

Circuit Training, A Different Kind of Workout

Circuit training is a different kind of workout. Choose as many techniques as you want to do in your workout. Techniques such as skipping rope, jab, left hook, right hook, straight right, slide and glide, etc. Decide upon an order you will do them in. For instance, if you choose to punch the heavy bag, skip rope, do your slide and glide, and your step and jab in that order, you now have the sequence of your circuit. Each technique is referred to as a station on that circuit. You do one round at each station in the order you previously chose. Once you have completed the circuit, go through it again as many times as you want. You can add a one minute rest round in between each working round or not, it's up to you. If you do not add the resting rounds, it is a harder workout. You still choose a focus for each round. Each station can have a specific focus, or you can pick a different focus each time you are at that station.

Ask the Coach

Do you think it is important to do my workouts on the same day every week, or is it OK to get them in whenever I get the chance?

Set up a workout schedule that is the same every week. For instance, decide to work out Monday, Wednesday, and Friday from 4 o'clock to 6 o'clock. When you have a consistent workout schedule, you will be more inclined to stick to it. When your workouts are harder than usual, because you are used to entering workout mode Monday, Wednesday, and Friday from 4 o'clock to 6 o'clock, you will have an easier time getting through the hard times instead of putting them off. Putting off the hard times will not get you anywhere but stuck.

I choose a focus but then I don't really know how to do it or make it happen.

A focus is just a mental concept at first. When you first assumed your BA, you probably intellectually understood that your feet were to be lined up under your hips and your hips lined up under your shoulders. But when you went to carry out this focus, it might suddenly have seemed confusing. By asking your mind to pay attention to the possibility of each focus, you start the process toward understanding it physically. Your body knows the correct, most efficient way to move. The ability to act on this knowledge may be buried, but it knows. Continue using your mind to keep the focus, and do what you can to act on the focus. Eventually your instinct, or what is often called body wisdom, will take over.

I've never done any kind of sports before, and I'm not a very aggressive person. Do you think boxing would be way out of my league?

No. If you're interested in trying it, go for it. Boxing is not strictly about aggression. It is about training and learning skills that will develop you mentally and physically. As long as you find your pace and stick to it, you will advance at precisely the right rate for you.

Things to Think About

Sweating is good for you. It flushes your system of toxins and cools you down when you get overheated. Sweating can also be a sign that you are upping your metabolism and working harder, which is an excellent way to shed excess fat. Many women feel it is unsightly to sweat, and this belief can inhibit your sweating process. If you feel this might be true for you, and you would like to sweat more, practice breathing deeper as you work out. Approach your workouts more vigorously, mentally imagining your pores opening up and releasing toxins.

Drinking water replenishes the fluids you sweat out. If you drink water during your workout be aware that it could give you side cramps. Drink less during your workout, then replenish your fluids after you are done. Get in the practice of drinking water during the day, especially in hot weather.

Eating less fat helps you shape a toned, flexible body. There are lots of fat free and fat reduced foods to choose from. Do not go on a strict diet in order to get "in shape." You just end up dieting instead of working out. When you work out be aware of using all of your body. That can be hard, sometimes. No one likes to admit they have a big derriere or stomach. Plus, it feels uncomfortable when the heavier parts of your body jiggle up and down. But all of you deserves being toned and shaped into muscle, so keep on moving. Just think what it will be like being able to put all of your weight behind your punches in the form of muscle power!

Stretching and Strengthening

Activity	Date									Focus
Folded Leg Stretch	Time									
	Reps									
Quadriceps Stretch	Time									
	Reps									
Hamstring Stretch	Time									
	Reps									
Triceps Stretch	Time									
	Reps									
Shoulder Stretch	Time									
	Reps									
Pectoral Stretch	Time									
	Reps									
Scorpion Tail	Sets									
	Reps									
Crunches	Sets									
	Reps									
Punch-ups	Sets									
	Reps									
Back-ups	Sets									
	Reps									
Leg Lift (Outside)	Sets									
	Reps									
Leg Lift (Inside)	Sets									
	Reps									
Triceps Extension	Sets									
	Reps									

NOTES _____

_____

NOTES _____

_____

NOTES _____

Table 10-1.
Workout Chart: Stretching and Strengthening.

Boxing Workout

Activity	Date									Focus
Stance	Time									
	RNDS									
Jump Rope	Time									
	RNDS									
Footwork: Advance & Retreat	Time									
	RNDS									
Footwork: Side to Side	Time									
	RNDS									
Footwork: Zig Zag	Time									
	RNDS									
Footwork: Mixed	Time									
	RNDS									
Straight Right	Time									
	RNDS									
Jab	Time									
	RNDS									
Step and Jab	Time									
	RNDS									
Hooks	Time									
	RNDS									
Mixed Punches	Time									
	RNDS									
Heavy Bag	Time									
	RNDS									
Speed Bag	Time									
	RNDS									

NOTES _____

_____

NOTES _____

_____

NOTES _____

Table 10-2.
Workout Chart: Boxing Workout.

Listening to Your Body

Balance comes through an awareness of being unbalanced and knowing how to regain balance from there.

As your old movement patterns are slowly replaced by a new sense of strength, you will feel some degree of discomfort. I discussed this in Chapter One. Discomfort is not critical. As you become more familiar with the new you, the discomfort will fade. As for troublesome aches and pains, boxing tends to relieve these because you are consistently aligning, stretching, and strengthening. A strong, aligned body is a content body. And yet it is not always easy to distinguish between discomfort and signals warning us of a potentially pre-injurious state. A pre-injurious state is when the body is being used in such a way that, if it continues, will eventually lead to injury. The reminders I provide in this chapter will help you distinguish between signs of discomfort and signals indicating a potentially preinjurious state. Refer to this chapter whenever you are not sure which one you are experiencing.

You want to listen to your body at all times. You use your body going to and from your car, sitting at your desk, taking a walk, hiking, biking, and paddling a canoe. Whenever you are using your body, you are receiving signals that tell you what is going on with it. Whether or not you know how to interpret those signals is another matter. For instance, if you are not used to exercising to the point of fatigue, the first time you skip rope you might not know what is going on. Your increasing heart rate could be interpreted as something that should be stopped. Actually it is good to exercise your heart. But you must get used to what it feels like when it starts pumping harder. As your panic around this sensation subsides, you find you can work at this level longer and longer each time. Eventually you feel sedentary if you do not get your weekly cardiovascular workout.

Listen to your body. Maybe you get winded easily, which makes skipping rope difficult. When you go at your own pace it's OK, but then you start feeling inept in comparison to other boxers, so you try to jump faster. Your body is telling you to slow down so you can develop good jump rope skills, while your mind is saying hurry up, get better faster. If you hurry up, you will either strain something or quit altogether. If your body says, "I've got to take this slow," take it slow.

Sometimes your body is ready to go for more and your mind hangs back, afraid. At these times your mind will pick up on signs of discomfort as a signal that you should stop working out. Bring your mind back to focusing on BA (Basic Alignment) so you can proceed into the discomfort zone. Discover what is really going on. It could be you are not so much tired as unused to feeling a new level of strength. Or perhaps you can feel some muscle that you have never felt before, and what you initially thought was pain turns out to be a new stretch. The process of balancing out the mental and the physical is an integral part of boxing. The more familiar you become with this process the more rewarding your workouts will be.

I worked with a boxer—Gale—who had trained in martial arts before she trained with me. She was remarkably fast and very powerful. It didn't take her long to alter her fighting style and learn to box. She trained hard. Her focus was fierce, razor sharp. She had good stamina, and she loved working out. She never got bored. She could practice the simplest move for a long time. Her mind was facile, she had a knack for perceiving strategy and putting together combinations. She pictured moves in her head and mimicked them. The problem was that she didn't know when to stop. She couldn't get enough training. She ran and played other sports. When she got injured she compensated by using another part of her body and by getting stronger. Her muscles became overly tight, reducing her flexibility. Yet she craved the sensations she got from working out.

Take time to familiarize yourself with what you are doing. Pay attention to where in your body you feel tension and where you don't. Your goal is an overall dynamic alertness to life.

It is hard to be moderate when you want to go all out. It can seem less challenging to stretch when you want to act. It is hard to go slow when you

want to go fast. It is scary to go fast when you need to go slow. You cannot have one without the other. By not taking the time to stretch, to slowly undo all the tension her body had built up, Gale slowly headed toward a major injury that would make her stop. But it was hard for her to know that. Who wants to stop feeling strong? Strength comes from developing all the areas of yourself and striking a balance. Listen to your body. It will tell you what is going on.

The Head and Neck

In our head-oriented world, it is not uncommon for us to lead with our heads or minds. This puts the neck in an unnatural position (see figure 11-1). This forward tilted position of the head and neck is detrimental to a boxer because it leaves him open to blows. This position also puts undue stress on your entire body.

Whenever you feel tension in your neck, think of your head as being drawn upward by a string. This allows the neck to return to its natural position, as an extension of the torso (see figure 11-2). This natural position is important to a boxer because when the head is drawn upwards toward the ceiling, the chin naturally tucks. No boxer wants to leave his chin open to a blow. When you punch make sure you are not leading with your head or chin. If you are, correct the position of your head and thus your neck.

Figure 11-1.
Stressing your neck.

Figure 11-2.
When the head is drawn upwards the chin naturally tucks.

The Face

Your face can tell you a lot about what you are feeling. You may find yourself grimacing when you work out. Generally grimaces indicate you are feeling afraid to keep going. Breathe deeply and bring your awareness back to your BA. On the other hand making "angry" faces can be helpful when you are gut level punching. An angry face can stir up aggression that can be used to fuel your punches.

Figure 11-3.
You do not want to punch with your shoulders up around your ears.

The Shoulders

I have discussed shoulders already. Aligning them is a major part of assuming BA. As a reminder, you will tend to punch from your shoulders at first. You will know you are doing this when your shoulders are up around your ears (see figure 11-3).

Also, if you experience shoulder pain, this is a good indication that you are punching with your shoulders up around your ears. When you experience shoulder pain, pause to bring your shoulders down into their correct BA position (see figure 11-4). Whenever you find yourself getting tense, pause to bring your shoulders down.

Figure 11-4.
Keep your shoulders down and back.

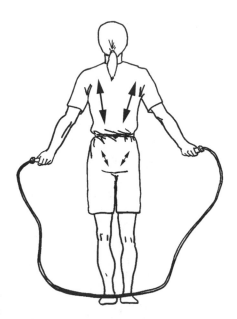

Figure 11-5.
Hold yourself with your lats and gluts.

The Chest

You may experience a tight feeling in your chest. Usually this means you need to breathe deeper, from your belly. Your body is asking for more oxygen and your lungs want to expand, but you are not used to consciously expanding them. This can make your chest feel tight. Also, open up your chest often. Punching with a closed chest can put undue stress on the chest muscles (see Chapter Seven to review the pectoral stretch).

The Elbows

I have mentioned before that you want to keep your elbows slightly bent when you strike the heavy bag. A hyperextended elbow hurts, and if you hyperextend it consistently, your elbow will become increasingly painful. Any kind of twinge in your elbows is a sign that you should pay immediate attention to keeping them slightly flexed when you punch.

Figure 11-6.
When you skip rope do not land with your weight on your knees.

The Wrists

Twinges in the wrists when striking the bag are not to be ignored. They mean you have struck the bag with your wrist bent either up, down, or to the side. Straighten it and keep it straight. Get a rubber ball and squeeze it minutes at a time. This will help strengthen your wrists and help you be aware of them. In your everyday life if your wrists hurt you, especially when lifting, make sure they are not unnecessarily bent.

The Back

Generally, back aches can be relieved by aligning. Assume BA, concentrate on holding yourself with your lats and gluts (see figure 11-5). If you experience lower back pain, more times than not your pelvis is tilted back. Align it forward so that your hips are over your feet and under your shoulders. Hold yourself erect with your imaginary side rods.

Figure 11-7.
Do not lock your knees.

The Knees

If your knees hurt when you jump rope it is generally because you are holding yourself in your knees (see figure 11-6). Automatically assume BA, making an effort to bring your weight down through your heels.

If your knees hurt in general you could be locking them (see figure 11-7). Keep your knees slightly flexed and alert (see figure 11-8).

When you are doing a hook and you feel twinges in your knee, you may not be remembering to pivot your foot with your punch. Practice pivoting your foot correctly.

Figure 11-8.
Keep your knees slightly flexed.

The Calves and Shins

When your calves hurt, stretch them out (see figure 11-9). First try to stay with the discomfort until you get a clearer picture of what is going on. Sometimes the calf muscles are not used to being worked as hard as footwork will work them. They start hurting, but it is more of a stretching into new strength than it is a pain that indicates injury. Your calves are going to get worked hard. Expect some discomfort as they get stronger, and if they cramp up, stretch them.

If your shins hurt stretch them out by bringing your foot off the floor and pointing your toes down until you feel a stretch along the shin. When you work out, focus on bringing your weight down through the back of your body instead of moving from the front of the body.

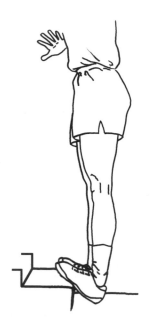

Figure 11-9.
Stretch your calves out if they cramp up.

Your Feet

If you get pain in your foot you could be overly stressing one part of your foot. Look at your feet in the mirror. Are they turned out or turned in? Do you stand mostly on the balls? Are your big toes raised up off the floor? Spend some time learning to distribute your weight evenly throughout your feet, from side to side and from the ball of your foot to your heel.

Practice foot alignment when you walk by initiating a heel to toe action with each step (see figure 11-10). Aligning your feet will help keep them healthy.

Figure 11-10.
When you walk place your feet heel to toe.

Ask the Coach

*Sometimes I get nause-
ated when I work out on
the heavy bag.*

When your mind jumps
ahead, you get more focused
on anticipating what might
happen than on what is
happening.

This can happen, and
generally it means you're
working hard, calling on
your reserves. Try to
stick it out to the end of
the round, remembering
to breathe deeply. As
you become more accustomed to this new level of
exertion, the nausea should cease.

*The outside of my thighs just below the hips hurts.
Is this OK?*

The muscles along the outside of the thigh are
often overly tight. All the punching, stretching,
and aligning you are doing is loosening them up.
Unfortunately the process of getting more range
of motion out of a muscle produces sensations
that are akin to growing pains. As these muscles
get stronger these pains will subside.

*For awhile my shoulders hurt, but I did what you
suggested and that helped. Then my left knee
started hurting. I worked on my BA and that went
away, too, but now my neck is hurting. Is there
such a thing as roving pain?*

During the period of realigning your body, each
new adjustment can affect you in a different part
of your body, which would account for the roving
pattern you're experiencing. Calmly note these
roving pains as you stick to your BA and to perfecting your moves. As you discover more and

more areas of new strength, they will eventually form an overall pattern of feeling strong and relaxed.

Things to Think About

Take delight in many things. Enjoy the feel of your favorite sweats as you pull them on. Wrap your hands carefully, knowing that they will be protected and strong. The texture of your jump rope is familiar, the grips fit into your palms. Even the moment waiting for the bell to ring is familiar. Thoughts about your day filter through as you wait, and when the bell goes, the familiar rhythm begins. Another workout, another chance to hone your skills.

As the rhythm takes over let an unsolved problem from your day hover just in front of you. For me it is a chapter from this manual. I have the points I want to make, but what's the order? As my breath comes a little quicker and my legs move through the initial heaviness they always go through when I jump rope, the problem of the day hovers. My arms are waking up, feeling a little tired, but that is their way of changing over from typing to boxing. Let your mind be the coach. Mine checks up on my alignment, tells me to bring my arms down a little, and still the problem of the day hovers. It is not exactly a focus, more a representation of feeling stuck.

As the workout progresses, as I continue to move past each little impulse to quit, the problem of the day cannot help but start to unravel. The first sweat breaks through my skin, bringing a pleasant rush of heat. I settle into the groove of movement. My feet remember what it is to flex and skip. My arms are connected again to my body. I wait in between rounds and start again. Now the groove of movement takes over. I'm along for the ride. In this place things seem simpler, somehow. The problem of the day is suddenly crystal clear. I can see the order of things, just as I can feel the familiar sensations of my feet against the mat, my wrists flicking the rope, my breath rushing in and out of my chest.

Appendix:
Boxing Resources

Equipment

Boxing Supplies

Ringside Inc.
P.O. Box 14171
Lenexa, KS 66285-4171
Telephone: (913) 888-1719
FAX: (913) 888-2198

You must get this catalog! Ringside is one of the main suppliers of boxing equipment.

Century Martial Arts Supply
1705 National Blvd
Midwest City, OK 73110
Telephone: (800) 626-2787
FAX: (800) 400 5485

This is a martial arts catalog but I really like their vinyl gloves because the price is right.

Active Apparel Group, Inc.
Everlast Woman
1350 Broadway, Suite 2300
New York, NY 10018
Telephone: (212) 239-0990
Fax: (212) 230-4261

Everlast Woman clothes are great looking, fun, and functional.

Amateur Boxing

United States

USA Boxing (United States Amateur Boxing, Inc.)
One Olympic Plaza
Colorado Springs, CO 80909-5776
Telephone: (719) 578-4506
FAX: (719) 632-3426

USA Boxing programs are open to both male and female athletes, ages 8 and up. These are the age groups:

Junior Division for ages 8 to 16.

Senior Division for ages 17 to 33.

Masters Division for all boxers 34 years and up. Matches are local only and there is no advancement. Masters may not compete against boxers under 34 years old.

Registration fees are set by your Local Boxing Committee and are usually $20. The first time you register you will need to provide a birth certificate, proof of permanent residency, or passport, and two pictures. A passbook is issued and must be presented every time a boxer competes. Registrations expire on June 30th of the year regardless of when you registered. Secondary sports insurance is included with the registration.

There are a few rule differences for amateur women boxers. Rounds last two minutes instead of three minutes. Breast protectors are required for all competitors; groin protectors are optional. Each female boxer must sign a waiver certifying that she is not pregnant.

The first US national championship for women was held in Augusta, Georgia, in July of 1997.

Local Boxing Committees:

Telephone numbers listed are those of the registration chairs. Call them to register.

Adirondack .... (518) 237-9279
Eastern New York State (See Niagara for Western NY)

Alaska .... See Pacific NW

Allegheny Mountain .... (412) 266-3066
Western Pennsylvania (See Middle Atlantic for Eastern PA)

Arizona .... (602) 849-9103

Arkansas.. (501) 225-7195

Border .... (915) 592-1435
Southwestern Texas

California Border .... (619) 744-2472
Southern California-San Diego area

Central California .... (209) 723-6755

Colorado .... (303) 296-6343

Connecticut .... (203) 229-2082

Florida .... (407) 632-5942

Florida Gold Coast .... (305) 731-1084
Southern Florida-Miami area

Georgia.. (912) 781-5886

Gulf.. (713) 675-9377
Eastern Texas-Houston area

Hawaii .... (808) 959-7902

Idaho Snake River .... (208) 345-2057
Southern Idaho and Far Eastern Oregon

Illinois .... (708) 446-4132
(See Ozark for Southern Illinois)

Indiana .... (317) 893-4226

Inland Northwest .... (509) 535-8969
Eastern Washington and Northern Idaho (See Pacific Northwest for
Western Washington)

Iowa .... (319) 394-3104

Lake Erie .... (216) 561-5697
Northeastern Ohio-Cleveland Area

Metropolitan .... (718) 829-6858
New York City area

Michigan .... (517) 791-1897

Middle Atlantic .... (717) 763-4595
Eastern Pennsylvania and Southern New Jersey

Minnesota .... (612) 434-1463

Missouri Valley .... (913) 294-4765
Kansas and Western Missouri (See Ozark for Eastern Missouri)

Montana .... (406) 761-2980

Nebraska .... (402) 721-8024

Nevada .... (702) 747-2853

New England .... (508) 588-7411
Massachusetts, New Hampshire, Rhode Island, and Vermont

New Jersey .... (201) 398-5175
Northern New Jersey (See Middle Atlantic for Southern New Jersey)

New Mexico .... (505) 327-1752

Niagara .... (315) 422-5365
Western New York (See Adirondack for Eastern NY)

North Carolina .... (704) 824-4002

North Dakota .... (701) 223-2920

Northern California .... (510) 372-7152

Ohio .... (419) 337-1518
(See Lake Erie for Northeastern Ohio)

Oklahoma .... (405) 364-0458

Oregon .... (503) 254-2933
(See Idaho Snake River for far Eastern Oregon)

Ozark .... (314) 535-4201
Eastern Missouri and Southern Illinois (See Missouri Valley for
Western Missouri)

Pacific Northwest .... (360) 792-9557
Western Washington (See Inland Northwest for Eastern Washington)

Potomac Valley .... (301) 568-3823
Washington, DC

South Atlantic... (410) 789-4411
Maryland

South Carolina .... (803) 873-9247

South Dakota... (605) 787-4438

South Texas .... (210) 923-0025

Southeastern .... (205) 828-3154
Tennessee, Alabama, and Florida panhandle

Southern .... (504) 654-6364
Louisiana and Mississippi

Southern California .... (714) 529-7047
Los Angeles area

Southwestern .... (214) 414-3708
Northeastern Texas-Dallas area

Utah... (801) 467-0539

Virginia.. (804) 527-2485

West Texas .... (915) 447-9414

West Virginia .... (606) 324-9483

Wisconsin.. (414) 282-0659

Wyoming .... (307) 347-3923

Canada

Canadian Amateur Boxing Association (CABA)
1600 James Naismith Drive
Gloucester, Ontario K1B 5N4
Telephone: (613) 748-5611
FAX: (613) 748-5740
E-mail: caba@boxing.ca

The Canadian Amateur Boxing Association held the first sanctioned women's amateur boxing match in North America in 1991 and continues to be very supportive of women boxers. CABA holds national female championships every year and its Female National Boxing Team represents Canada internationally.

Canadian rules are similar to US rules in that you must contact the provincial association to register as an amateur boxer. Here are the phone numbers for these organizations.

Provincial/Territorial Associations:

Alberta A.B.A. .... (403) 453-8563

British Columbia A.B.A. .... (604) 291-7921

Manitoba A.B.A. .... (204) 925-5658

New Brunswick A.B.A. .... (506) 382-2195

Newfoundland A.B.A. .... (709) 722-6145

Boxing Nova Scotia .... (902) 425-5450

Boxing Ontario .... (416) 426-7250

Fed. Quebecoise de Boxe .... (514) 252-3047

P.E.I. A.B.A. .... (902) 628-1596

Saskatchewan A.B.A. .... (306) 652-9411

Yukon A.B.A. .... (403) 633-4858

International

The bylaws of the Association Internationale de Boxe Amateur (AIBA), the international amateur boxing association, allow women boxers to compete internationally. We all look forward to the possibility of women's boxing at the 2004 Olympics.

Amateur Boxing Officials

Anyone can become a boxing judge or referee by taking the appropriate exams. Contact your Local Boxing Committee if you want more information.

Recreational and Fitness Boxing

Contact local health clubs and gyms for boxing programs offered in your area.

Professional Boxing

There are a growing number of women boxing professionally and you can see professional boxing matches on TV or attend a local event. Contact one of these professional boxing organizations for more information about registering as a professional boxer.

International Female Boxers Association
Jackie Kallen, Commissioner
655 Deep Valley Dr, Suite 110
Rolling Hills Estates, CA 90274
Telephone: (310) 541-1206

Women's International Boxing Federation
Barbara Buttrick, President
PO Box 398123
Miami Beach, FL 33239
Telephone: (305) 531-0380

Suggested Reading

Andre, Sam and Nat Fleischer. *A Pictorial History of Boxing.* Citadel Press, 1987.
This book is a history of male professional boxers, from the bare knuckle days to the present. It has hundreds of photos and covers all of the weight divisions. (But no women!)

Chandler, David, John Gill, Tania Guha, and Tawadros, eds. *Boxer: An Anthology of Writings on Boxing and Visual Culture.* The MIT Press, 1996.
This is a stunning book, full of boxing photos and graphics. The essays cover many aspects of boxing, including one essay on women in boxing.

Dempsey, Jack. *Championship Fighting:Explosive Punching and Aggressive Defense.* Edited by Jack Cuddy. Centerline Press, 1983.
Jack Dempsey, a champion heavyweight in the 1920s, covers the art of punching and defense.

Denfeld, Rene. *Kill The Body The Head Will Fall.* Warner Books, 1997.
Denfeld highlights her experiences as an amateur boxer, and voices her opinions on what it means for a woman to box.

DePasquale, Peter. *The Boxer's Workout.* Fighting Fit, 1990.
A workout book for the male, white collar boxer.

Kallen, Jackie. *Hit Me With Your Best Shot : How to Score a Knockout in All of Life's Arenas.* St. Martins, 1997.
Kallen is the commissioner of the International Female Boxers Association. She is also a professional boxing manager.

Lee, Bruce. ***Tao of Jeet Kune Do.*** Ohara Publications, 1993.
The Tao of Jeet Kune Do is Bruce Lee's view on life and the fighting arts. This book is an excellent source of inspiration, philosophy, fighting technique, and lore.

Miller, Davis. ***The Tao of Muhammad Ali.*** Warner Books, 1996.
A wonderful tribute to one of the greatest athletes to ever live.

Oates, Joyce Carol. ***On Boxing.*** Ecco Press, 1994.
In these essays Oates explores the impact of boxing on our society.

Olajide, Michael, Jr. with Phil Berger. ***Aerobox.*** Warner Books, 1995.
A noncontact aerobic program and total workout for men and women.

Plimpton, George. ***Shadow Box.*** Lyons & Burford, 1993.
George Plimpton, sports writer and editor, gives a candid account of the professional boxing world through an amateur's eyes.

Plummer, William. ***Buttercups and Strong Boys.*** Penguin USA, 1990.
A knockout of a book. It tells the tales of East Harlem kids who train for the New York Golden Gloves. Out of print, but worth tracking down.

Index

A

B

Check out our web site!

http://www.girlbox.com/

The *Boxing For Everyone* web site lists up to date information and other stuff that we couldn't fit in this book. Check our site for information on:

- boxing web sites

- boxing gyms

- training programs

- upcoming events

- more "Ask The Coach" questions and answers

The *Boxing For Everyone* web site lists other boxing publications from AmandaLore Publishing. For additional information send a message to **info@girlbox.com**.

Order Form

Telephone orders: U.S. Toll Free   (888) 240-1934
                               International orders   (206) 320-1381

Fax orders: (206) 320-9374

On-line orders: sales@girlbox.com or http://www.girlbox.com/

Postal orders: AmandaLore Publishing
                      1111 E Madison St, Suite 433-265
                      Seattle, WA 98122

Please send me _____ copies of *Boxing For Everyone: How To Get Fit and Have Fun With Boxing* at $19.95 plus $3.00 shipping and handling for a total of $22.95 per book.

Name:_____

Address:_____

City:_____ State:_____ Zip:_____

Telephone:_____ Email:_____

Sales Tax:
Please add 8.6% for books shipped to Washington state addresses (each book, including Washington state tax and shipping, is $24.67).

Shipping:
Your book will be shipped either UPS or USPS Priority Mail. For overnight shipping add $10.00.

Payment:
Check: please make your check payable to AmandaLore Publishing in U.S. dollars.

Credit Card: ____VISA ____Mastercard
Card Number:_____ Exp. date: ____/____
Name on card:_____

Call toll free and order now!